PLAYBOY
XX-CUPP

Translation / Leona Wong
Editing / W. Johns
Lettering / Shelby Peak
Graphic Design / W. Johns

™ 801 Media, Inc.
www.801media.com
contact@801media.com

ISBN-10: 1-934129-12-7
ISBN-13: 978-1-934129-12-8
First edition printed November 2007

10 9 8 7 6 5 4 3 2 1

Printed in China

HEY,
WANT ME TO READ YOUR PALM?
MY NAME IS KAZUYA SAKAI (AGE 23, SCAFFOLD CONSTRUC-TOR).
生意気
...I'M NOT YOUR STEPPIN' STONE...
SHAMELESS
AND I HAVE A TUTOR.
REALLY?
YOU KNOW HOW?
FOR SOME REASON...

FOR THE FIRST TIME IN MY LIFE, I'M PUMPED FOR A TEST...
「生意気。」
なまいき
I'M NOT YOUR STEPPIN' STONE
SHAMELESS
LOVE

HMM...
A LONG LIFE LINE...
AND YOU'RE VERY QUICK-TEMPERED.
AS FOR MARRIAGE...
NOT HAPPENING.
WHAT?
NO WAY!
I WAS TOLD I'M GONNA MARRY EARLY!
REALLY?
OKAY, GIVE ME YOUR RIGHT HAND.
BOTH?
YES, BOTH...

OY, MASASHI ...
COME ON, IPPA-CHI* ...
JUST ONCE...
*SEE TRANSLATOR AND EDITOR NOTES.
IT ALL STARTED THREE MONTHS AGO.
I WAS BUILDING THE ADDITION TO MASASHI EZUMI'S HOUSE...
WHAT DO YOU WANT WITH MY SISTER?
NO, JUST THAT... UM...

I WAS JUST WONDERING IF NATSUKO-CHAN HAS A BOY-FRIEND ...
...OR SOMETHING.
...
YOU KNOW.
AREN'T YOU GETTING AHEAD OF YOURSELF?
YOU'RE SMALLER THAN HER, TOO.
IT DEPENDS ON YOUR ACADEMIC BACK-GROUND.
ARE YOU A COLLEGE DROPOUT?
THAT'S SOMETHING I DON'T LIKE TO ADMIT. I'VE BEEN WORKING FOR EIGHT YEARS NOW.
BUT TILL...

I WAS FROZEN BY THOSE WORDS.
I'M SORRY... FOR BEING SMALL ...
WORDS FROM THE PROUD HONOR STUDENT...
ATTENDEE OF FAMOUS SCHOOL
FLOURISHING YOUTH AT SEVENTEEN.
HEIGHT: 6'1"
AND I'M SORRY FOR ONLY HAVING A JUNIOR HIGH DIPLOMA!
SO BEGAN THE ABUSE OF MY WEAKER POINTS.
LICK ME...
TURN AROUND.
MONO
SO THEN...

WHAT THE FUCK AM I DOING?
AFTER THAT...
I DIDN'T SAY A WORD. AND IN THE REGS OF EFEAT, I THOUGHT I...

I CAN'T LET IT END LIKE THIS FOR ME!!
YOU'RE TAKING THE EXAMS ...?!
AIM FOR A HIGH SCHOOL DIPLO-MA.
MY PROBLEMS BEGAN THERE.
FIRST OFF, SELF-STUDY IS *IMPOSSIBLE* FOR YOU.
AFTER PASSING, YOU'D GO TO SCHOOL PART TIME... IS THAT TOO MUCH?

HOWEVE
I AM WILLI
DO YOU A
FAVOR AN
TUTOR YO
DOOM
I DIDN'T LIKE HOW HE SAID IT, BUT THERE WASN'T ANYONE ELSE I COULD TURN TO.
SINCE THE GUYS I KNOW ARE...
ARE ALL LIKE THIS.
NAME A KIND OF CELL.
ANS. A JAIL CELL.
DID I TOUCH YOUR HARP STRINGS?
WARNING
HE MEANT HEART-STRINGS.
ABOVE ALL ...
GAH
I'VE NEVE BACKED DOWN FROM ANYTHING THAT I'VE SAI I'D DO.
NEVER!
WAH HA HA HA HA
WAH?!
AND SO.
LIKE NOW?

HEY.
IT'S LIKE...
THIS WAS WHAT HE WANTED AS TU-ITION.
WHERE THE HELL DID YOU LEARN THAT, BASTARD?
RUB
IT'S THERE FOR A REASON.
SUCK
WHAT THE HELL ARE YOU...
AH!
YOU SAY THAT ...
YOU KNOW YOU LIKE IT...
CAN... I FUCK YOU?
NO FUCKING WAY!
THERE'S SOMETHING WRONG WITH THAT SHARP MIND OF HIS.
OR IS IT JUST ME?
THEN KEEP SUCKING.
GLARE

JOLT
I'M NOT USED TO THIS BUT...
AH...
IPPACHI ...
IT'S NOT ALL BAD.
TWITCH TWITCH
I THINK ...
I'M...
COMING ...
QUIVER
JOLT
THERE'S SOMETHING ABOUT HIS PRIMITIVE CHARM.
WHEN YOU SAID FAVOR...

SHUT UP.
LET ME CONCENTRATE.
DOES HE HAVE A SUPERIORITY COMPLEX?
IT'S STRANGE.
コンコン
KNOCK KNOCK...
ANIKI, I'M COMING IN.
OPEN

OH? YOU'R LEAVIN SO SOON
NA...
NACCHAN ... ♥
SORRY! LOOKS LIKE I'M A BIT TOO LATE.
I JUST MADE THIS...
HUH...
DOES IT SMELL STRANGE IN HERE?
NAT-SUKO.
YOU WERE THE ONE SAYING HOW BAD IT WAS BECAUSE IPPACHI-SAN DOESN'T HAVE AIR CONDITIONING AT HOME.
I'M SORRY, IPPACHI-SAN!
I TOL YOU N TO GO ANY TROUBL
I HAVE EVERYTHING I NEED FOR TUTORING IN MY ROOM ALREADY, SO DON'T DO IT AGAIN.
GEEZ, ANIKI...
NACCHAN... ♥
FIDGET
NO, NO...
FIDGET

HMPH.
WELL THAT'S JUST HOW I AM.
MASASHI?
YOU...
I GUESS HE'S SELF-CONSCIOUS...
THANKS FOR HAVING ME!
OY, IPPACHI.
IS HE HERE FOR YOU?
OH.
WHAT'S UP? ♪

PICKI ME L WIT YOU RIDE
NO...
JUST PASSING BY.
AW, THERE YOU GO AGAIN.
BEING ALL SHY. ♡
WAIT FOR ME. I'M ALMOS DONE.
I LOVE, LOVE THE AIR CONDITIONING AT YOUR PLACE.
ACTUALLY.
I HA TO TUTO YOU YOU PLAC TODA
WE HAVE GUESTS OVER.
BUT THE AC!
GEH
...
THEN WE'LL JUST SKIP TODAY.
STARE
OKAY, FINE!
I DON'T NEED CRAP FROM YOU. THE SUN'S GONNA BE HELL AT MY PLACE THOUGH.
IS IT MESSY?
YUP, YOU HELP CLEAN.

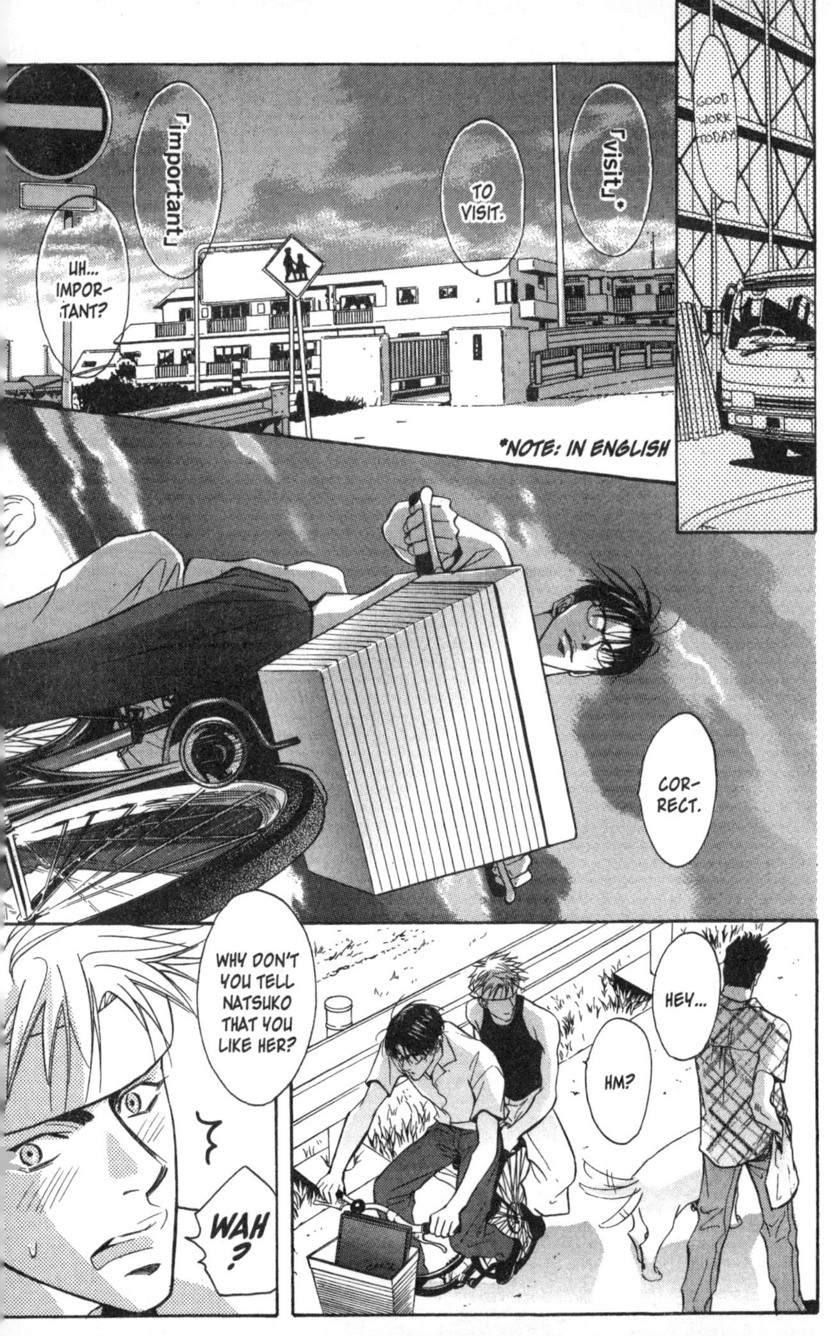
GOOD WORK TODAY
「visit」*
TO VISIT.
「important」
UH... IMPORTANT?
*NOTE: IN ENGLISH
CORRECT.
HEY...
HM?
WHY DON'T YOU TELL NATSUKO THAT YOU LIKE HER?
WAH?

IT'S,
JUST THAT YOU DON'T HAVE TO WAIT TILL YOU TAKE THE TEST. SHE KNOWS HOW HARD YOU'RE WORKING.
THAT'S NOT IT.

WHAT?
...

I'M AFRAID OF REJEC-TION.
A STUD LIKE YOU WON'T UNDERSTAND.
...

YOU'RE RIGHT, I DON'T.
GOOD FOR YOU, BASTARD.
YOU DIDN'T HAVE TO SAY IT.
IT'S BE-CAUSE ...
I'VE NEVER BEEN IN LOVE.
HUH?
LIKE I SAID.

THAT'S WHY I'VE NEVER BEEN DUMPED EITHER.
AREN'T YOU...
A BIT TOO SERIOUS?
WHAT HAPPENED TO YOUR YOUTH?
HA HA HA HA.
IT'S NOT FUNNY.
OH WELL.
SPRING WILL COME AGAIN FOR YOU SOMEDAY.
OKAY?
ARE YOU TRYING TO MAKE ME FEEL BETTER?
...
LIKE I SAID...
BUT IT'S SUMMER... RIGHT?!
WHAT KIND OF "SPRING" IS THIS?
UM... MASASHI-KUN?

IT'S FINE ... PAYING IN ADVANCE OCCASION-ALLY.
HE STRIPPED.
OKAY!!
CAN WE AT LEAST TAKE A BATH FIRST?!
WHAT?
IT'S SO HOT, I CAN'T HEAR YOU.
HEY, HEY.
EVEN THOUGH YOU'RE LIKE THIS.
THAT'S BE-CAUSE ...
REMEMBER OUR CONDITIONS?
EH HEH HEH.
MA-SASHI?

?!
MN...
UGH...
YOU KNOW ...
IF YOU DON'T LIKE THE PERSON YOU DO IT WITH, IT'S MEANINGLESS.
OH?

YOU WANT TO DO STUFF LIKE THIS WITH NATSUKO
I'LL DO IT!
I'LL TAKE IT OFF MYSELF!
WHOA, WHOA!
WAIT.
MASA...
EH?
BLUSH
THEY WON'T COME OFF...
THESE BOXERS...
DON'T TEAR MY FAVORITE PAIR.
TCH...
THAT...
STOP... THAT...

HA
WHAT WOULD "THAT" BE?
AH...
SLICK
MY ASS ...
YOUR ASS?
FIN-GERS ...
AH!
AH...
JOLT
DRIP
DRIP
DRIP
TREMBLE
TREMBLE
HERE?
YOU LIKE IT HERE?
SLIP
SHIT...
MARIA TANAKA
HAA...

WHAT THE HELL IS THIS ...
MARIA TANAKA
NO...
I'M GONNA ... SOON...
SO MUCH SWEAT ...
IT'S DRIPPING HERE, TOO...
SO SLIPPERY HERE...
JUST LIKE A GIRL.
SHIT...
EVERYTHING'S...
THIS IS EX-ACTLY LIKE ...

SEX.
W-
HUH?!
WAIT.
MASASHI.
THERE'S SOMETHING WRONG ABOUT THIS!
I CAN'T DO THIS WITH ANOTHER GUY!
MARIA TANAKA
WHAT ARE YOU TALKING ABOUT?
THEN WHAT THE HELL HAVE WE BEEN DOING ALL THIS TIME?!

TCH...
WHAT?
CH...
IT'S IN...
HA
SOME-THING LIKE THIS...
SHIVER
DAMN ...
SHIVER
THIS IS SO MUCH BETTER.
HOW THE HELL SHOULD I HAVE KNOWN?

YOU TOO...
KAZUYA!
AH!
KAZUYA...
HAA!
WHAT THE HELL?
HAA...
THRUST
THRUST
AH!
THRUST
KAZUYA!
I'M...
COMING!
AH!

WHAT THE HELL ARE YOU TRYING TO DO?
MARIA TANAKA
...TCH.
ピンポーン
DING DONG

ピンポーン!!
DING DONG
COMING!
OPEN
AH, IPPACHI-SAN!
HEY!
MY BROTHER'S STILL OUT.
YOU WANNA WAIT INSIDE?
NO... I MEAN, TODAY ...
HEY ...
I NEED TO TALK TO YOU...
ME?
WHAT IS IT?
GIGGLE
NA-NA-NACCHAN, I KNOW YOU LIKE SMART GUYS, BUT...
AND THAT'S NOT ME AT ALL, BUT UM... AND I HAVE NO MONEY, BUT UH WELL...
SURPRISED
HUH...?
CLATTER

IS A JUNIOR HIG GRADUATE NOT GOOD ENOUGH...?
...
IPPACHI-SAN...
IS THIS WHAT I...
I...
I REALLY...
LIKE YOU.
SCREECH

ANIKI
...
...!
TELL HIM, NATSUKO
...
THAT YOU'RE NOT INTO UGLY FOOLS LIKE HIM.
MASASHI ?!
IT'S USELESS.
I KNOW WHAT SHE LIKES.
AFTER SEEING THAT STUPID FACE OF YOURS, I JUST HAD TO MESS WITH YOU.
...WHAT?!

THEN YO
FOLLOWE
ALONG.
IT WAS GREAT FUN.
TAKING THE EXAMS?
HEH
IS IT NORMAL TO GO THAT FAR FOR A GIRL?
THAT'S WHY YOU'RE SO STUPID!
ANIKI!
AND FOR A GIRL LIKE HER!
HA HA HA HA
BAS-TARD...
FUCK YOU!!
PUNCH
CLATTER
IPPACHI-SAN!!

APOLO-GIZE.
APOLOGIZE TO HER!
YOU'RE THE STUPID ONE!
TCH...
YOU'RE THE UGLY ONE!
THAT'S ENOUGH, IPPACHI-SAN!
YOU DON'T NEED TO TELL ME.
I'M TRASH.
I KNOW THAT BEST.
I'D HAVE TO, AT THIS POINT.
CRACK

I KNOW OF AT LEAST ONE LOVE.
MASASHI?
SORRY, BUT YOU'LL HAVE TO DO YOUR BEST ON THAT TEST YOUR-SELF.
BUT...YOU MIGHT NOT HAVE TO, ANYMORE.
WAIT, ANIKI... WHERE ARE YOU GOING?
MASASHI!
HOW SHOULD I KNOW?
SORRY, NACCHAN, I HAVE TO...
AH... OKAY...
IT'S TOO COMPLICATED FOR ME.
MA-SASHI!
HOLD ON!

THE REASON YOU MADE FUN OF ME...
MASASHI!
!
WAH!
DON'T YOU THINK...
YOUR METHODS ARE STRANGE?
SHUDDER
THAT HURT...

IPPACHI-SAN
YOU'RE...
VERY VIOLENT...
SORRY.
HEY.
WHAT YOU SAID...
WHAT DID YOU MEAN?
WHAT?

"TRASH."
LONG STORY.
BUT THAT MUST BE IT.
WHAT?
MY COMPLEX.
MY JEALOUSY OF NATSUKO.
IT STARTED A LONG TIME AGO.
"SO BRIGHT, SO KIND, BIG-HEARTED, A GOOD CHILD".
IT WAS NEVER TO ME.
I'VE HAD A BAD ATTITUDE SINCE. BUT I'VE ONLY NOTICED IT RECENTLY.
...
AFTER MEETING YOU...

IT'S BECAUSE
YOU CHOSE HER.
...?!
I DIDN'T LIKE THAT.
AND THEN YOU DECIDED TO TAKE THE EXAMS FOR HER.
DOES THAT MEAN...
NO WAY.
...
WAIT A SEC.
YOU ACTUALLY...
IT MEANS ...

YOU'RE SLOW.
IS HE SERI-OUS?
SO THIS IS...
IPPA-CHI...?
RUSTLE
JUST THAT DAMNED SIMPLE?
YOU'RE SUCH AN IDIOT.
ISN'T THERE ANOTHER WAY?
YOUR APPROACH IS...
HOW COULD I?
YOU WOULDN'T CARE FOR ANOTHER GUY.
NOT TRUE...
WELL, NOT TRUE NOW.

I CAN'T LEAVE YOU ALONE.
SERIOUSLY... AND YOU AREN'T EVEN MY TYPE.
WHOOSH
HEY?
I LIKE YOU...
I LIKE YOU...
I REALLY DO.
THAT'S NOT FAIR...

SUCH INNOCENT WORDS...
COMING FROM THAT MOUTH.
TCH...
SHAKE
SORRY... DOES IT HURT?
HA
HA
DON'T...
PULL OUT...
MORE THAN ANY-THING ...
MY BODY RE-SPONDS TO HIM...
PUSH
SLIP
RIGHT THERE ...
HAA
DON'T STOP...
HAA...
HAA...
AH...
AHH...
I KNOW THAT.

I FELL IN LOVE...
THE REAL REASON I'M TAKING THE EXAMS...
IS STILL A SECRET ...
"MY COMPLE FOR YOU"
WHAT?
YOU'RE STILL TAKING THE TEST ?!
YEAH, OF COURSE.
WHY?!
IF IT'S STILL FO NATSUKO
THE MAN, IPPACHI, NEVER GOES BACK ON HIS WORD!
SO YOU'LL KEEP PAYING ME FOR TUTOR-ING?
YOU ARE THE MAN.
LEER
NATSUKO AT THE TIME.
SHE ACTUALLY HAS A BOYFRIEND.
HMPH
WELL, THAT'S FINE.
STOP IT! DON'T DO THAT!
生意気。~I'M NOT YOUR STEPPIN' STONE end
SHAMELESS.

I'M NOT YOUR
「生意気。て」
STEPPIN' STONE
SHAMELESS
恋していると言ってくれ
TELL ME YOU'RE IN LOVE

であるから
x² + y² + z² = 69 …③
①②から
x = −2y, z = −2y …④
WHAT'S THIS?
YOU'RE WET DOWN HERE, TOO?
THIS IS, OF COURSE, SIXTY-NINE.
I CAN BOTH SPELL AND DO IT.
YOU... LIAR...
HAA
HA
NOT POSSIBLE...
YOU'RE... LICKING IT... ALL UP.
AND SO, SEXUALITY IS ANOTHER HURDLE I'VE OVERCOME.

YOU'RE ALMOST THERE...
TWITCH
AH...
SPLSH
AHH...
HNG.
QUIVER
QUIVER
FLICK
LICK
LICK
HAA... AH!
I WANT TO GET EVEN TODAY.
MASASHI...
NO, DON'T COME YET...
HA
HAA
SWIVEL
WHEN!!
AND I HAVE MY WAYS!
I'LL WIN!
RUB
UH?!
WHA, MASASHI!

THRUST
GUH?!
HAA
HA
AH...
MA... MASA... SHI!
OW...
THAT HURTS!
TAKE IT OUT!
PUSH PUSH
IDIOT!
IT'S FINE.
I'M NOT ACTING!
YOU KNOW I WOULDN'T!
BUT YOU'LL HAVE TO GET USED TO IT, RIGHT?
JUST PULL IT OUT!
THRUST
NO, DAMN IT!
NOT TO THIS!
PUSH

IT FUCKING HURTS, GET OUT!!
YOU DICK ALIEN!
CRACK
PFFT
KAZUYA SAKAI, MY LOVER WHO IS SIX YEARS OLDER AND IS A HARDWORKING SCAFFOLD CONSTRUCTOR.
DICK ALIEN...
AMN
PPA-
CHI...
THE TRUTH IS...
I COULDN'T HAVE MY WAY WITH HIM.

HOW HUMILI-ATING...
SIGH...
THEN YOU UN-DERSTAND MY SENTI-MENTS,
EZUMI.
ALGEBRA HAS ENDED ALREADY.
TREMBLE TREMBLE
CLASSIC LITERATURE
ALGEBRA & GEOMETRY
DID YOU CHANGE YOUR SCHOOL SELEC-TION?
SATOU...
IT'S SAITOU.

WHAT'S WRONG WITH YOU?
SPACING OUT AT SUCH A CRITICAL TIME... THE CLASS IS SHOCKED.
YAMAUCHI ISN'T GOING TO LET IT GO.
...
GEEZ... WE'VE BEEN TO-GETHER SINCE MIDDLE SCHOOL!
JUST RE-MEMBER ALREADY!
I DON'T RECALL BEING TOGETH-ER.
EZUMI.
I'M WORRIED ABOUT YOU.
WE'RE ALL IN THIS TOGETHER. I THOUGHT *YOU* AT LEAST WOULDN'T GIVE UP...
HOW CAN YOU LOSE TO *ME?* YOUR RANK DROPPED TO THE TWO-DIGIT RANGE...
SOME-THING MUST'VE HAPPENED.
NOT REALLY.

WE'RE ONLY SECOND YEARS. IT'S OKAY TO DROP A LITTLE OCCASIONALLY.
ARE YOU SERIOUS?!
DIDN'T... DIDN'T YOU WANT TO GO TO TOKYO UNIVERSITY WITH ME?!
TO NOT REPEAT A YEAR AND SUCCEED TOGETHER!!
WASN'T THAT OUR GOAL?!
OUR...?
TOKYO UNIVERSITY?
WHEN DID I SAY ANY OF THAT?
THIS GUY IS SCARY.
HEY, SAIKI...
PURPOSELY
IT'S SAITOU!
SAITOU ...
DON'T YOU THINK YOU NEED TO RELAX ONCE IN A WHILE, TOO?
WHA.
THAT'S NOT WHAT I MEAN...
YOU PROPOSE THAT I SLACK OFF?!

YOU'RE TOO UP-TIGHT.
IT'S OKAY TO LOVE YOURSELF SOMETIMES. ★
?!
NOT SLACK OFF. JERK OFF.
OKAY?
NO...
WAY...
OH.
I CAN SEE YOUR UVULA **HANGING**.
BUDDY.
NOOOO!
GEEZ...
I SAID UVULA...

STUDYING DOESN'T HELP AT ALL...
BRIIIING
LIKE I SAID.
HEH
PI IS THE MEANING OF WHITE DAY.
YUP.
THEN, WHAT DOES BLUE DAY MEAN?!
HUH?!
WHAT THE HELL IS THAT?
BLUE DAY?
WHAT? YOU DON'T KNOW WHAT BLUE DAY IS?
SMIRK SMIRK
WHA... WHAT IS IT? TELL ME!
IS IT ON THE TEST?!
POINT
THAT'S NOT GOOD!
WAH HA HA...
安全第一

BLUE DAY. IN OTHER WORDS, A GLOOMY DAY.
GUYS WHO DON'T GET ANYTHING ON VALENTINES DAY CALL IT A BLUE DAY.
(THIS IS A LIE.)
AH!
MASASHI!
RING RING
SO THAT MEANS THE WHOLE YEAR COUNTS AS A BLUE DAY FOR YOU GUYS!
HEH HEH HEH
SMIRK
HA HA HA
OH WELL...
DIFFERENT GENERATION
REALLY, MASHI.
CAN THIS GUY REALLY PASS THE EXAMS?
OF COURSE I CAN.
MASHI?!
I HAVE GREAT TEACHER MASASHI'S APPROVAL!
NOT MY APPROVAL, BUT MY HANDS ON YOU...
BA-BUMP
SQUEEZE SQUEEZE

MY REASONING IS THAT NEXT SPRING WHEN HE GOES TO SCHOOL PART TIME, THE POSSIBILITY THAT HE'LL ASK ME TO TUTOR HIM IS...
NONE.
TO BE EXACT, THERE'S NO REASON THAT HE'D NEED ME...
BUT, YOU'RE TOO NICE.
MUST TO BE A PAIN TO DO IT FOR FREE.
MORE LIKE YOU NEED EXTREME PATIENCE.
NORMALLY.
NO, I DO GET PAID.
GEH
YOU...
HEH
IDIOT... YOU CAN'T CALL...
A BACK RUB PAYMENT!
HUH?!
BACK RUB?
LAME!
GAHAHA!
YOU THINK HE'S YOUR MOM OR SOMETHING?
PAY THE GUY IN CASH!
SHUT UP!!

DAMN IT...
HURRY AND MOVE ALREADY!
WAH HA HA
THIS IS A "BACK RUB"?
HEH HEH
QUIT IT...
I HAVE TO STUDY, OR ELSE...
OH? YOU'RE BEING GOOD TODAY?
IS IT BECAUSE OF WHAT HAPPENED EARLIER?
WATCH IT.

SHOWING IT OFF WITH A HUGE BANDAGE...
THAT'S DIRTY.
WELL... I *AM* A DICK ALIEN...
THAT'S NASTY!
WELL, MY DICK IS PRETTY DANGER-OUS...
YOU'RE FREAKING AGGRES-SIVE!!
YOU DON'T HAVE TO SAY THAT TWICE!
TAKE THIS THING OFF... AND LET'S KISS...
DON'T PRE-TEND TO BE NICE.
COME ON...
WE'RE LOVERS, RIGHT?
IF THAT'S THE CASE...
?

THEN DON'T CALL IT A "PAY-MENT."
THAT SOUNDS... DIRTY.
IPPACHI...
TACKLE
GUH?!
HA
MASASHI, WAIT...
HA...
WHAT IS WRONG WITH YOU?!
HA...
"PUT IT IN HALF HARD,
SO IT CAN GROW INSIDE..."
HUH?!
SO IT WON'T HURT THAT WAY...
WHAT... WELL THAT'S PERFECTLY APPROPRIATE, HUH?!
HAA
HAA
HA...

I READ IT IN A REFERENCE BOOK. IT MUST BE TRUE... RIGHT?!
HAA
HAA...
HA
SHUT UP! I'LL NEVER TRUST A DICK ALIEN!
RUSTLE RUSTLE
CONDOM... CAN WE SKIP IT TODAY?
HAA...
HA...
WE'VE NEVER USED ONE BEFORE!
AH... MASASHI!
SERIOUS-LY?! THAT'S TOO SUDDEN!
OW...
IT HURTS!
OW! OW!
?!
FORCE
AH!
STOP...
HAA...
IT HURTS ...
OW!
HA...
HEY!!
HA...
OW...

ARE YOU FUCKING EVEN HARD YET?!
PFFT
KICK
BULLY-ING? NO WAY...
ANIKI... ARE YOU OKAY?
WHAT ON EARTH ...?!
SMOLDER...
SMOLDER
SMOLDER
DON'T TELL MOM AND DAD.
PPACHI ...

HE LIKED MY SISTER IN THE BEGINNING.
I WAS JUST WONDERING IF NATSUKO-CHAN HAS A BOY-FRIEND...
HE FIRST SAW HER WHEN HE WAS WORKING ON OUR HOUSE FOR A SCAF-FOLDING COMPANY.
I COULDN'T STAND IT, SO I PROVOKED HIM.
AREN'T YOU GETTING AHEAD OF YOURSELF?
YOU'RE SMALLER THAN HER, TOO.
THE JAB ABOUT HIS EDUCATION IRKED HIM THE MOST.
SO, SIMPLE-MINDED IPPACHI GOT IT INTO HIS HEAD TO TAKE THE EXAMS.
MIDDLE SCHOOL GRADUATE.
THEN, I MADE MYSELF HIS TUTOR.
RUSTLE
I HAVE NOT LOST MY MIND.
BUT FOR SOME REASON...

I FELL IN LOVE WITH HIM.
THAT'S WHY...
I COULDN'T GET OVER HIS LOVE FOR NATSUKO.
IT WAS A WONDER HOW HE JUST ACCEPTED MY REQUEST FOR PAYMENT SO INNOCENTLY.
...
FOR IPPACHI......
WAIT. MASASHI.
THERE'S SOME-THING WRONG ABOUT THIS!
HE NEVER THOUGHT IT WAS SEX EVEN UP TO THAT POINT.
IN
...

HE DIDN'T EVEN KNOW WHAT I WANTED...
MAYBE EVEN NOW...
IT'S JUST SOME-THING THAT FLOATS BY HIM.
SHIT.
DAMN IPPACHI ...
AND AT TH TIME.
HE FELT EVERY-THING, TOO...
I CAN'T LEAVE YOU ALONE.
SERI-OUSLY... AND YOU AREN'T EVEN MY TYPE.
IT'S TOO LATE TO SAY THAT IT WAS ALL A LIE.
INHALE
I...

I LIKE YOU...
SO MUCH...
HA
I CAN'T STAND IT.
HA
IPPACHI ...
RUB
RUB
IPPACHI ...
YEAH! SEE YOU LATER!
NO MATTER HOW MUCH I IGNORE IT...
HA...
TCH...
I COULD HEAR YOUR VOICE.
A SICK BASTARD LIKE ME...
SQUELCH
SLICK
DRIP
HAA...

IPPACHI ...
IP...
I'VE FALLEN FOR YOU WITHOUT EVEN REALIZING IT.
MASASHI...
MASASHI ...
MASASHI...
SPURT
JOLT
JOLT
I'M GONNA COME... INSIDE...
SPURT
TWITCH
SHOCK
JOLT
JOLT

TCH...
HA...
HA...
IPPACHI...
?
WHO ARE YOU?
PLEASE...
PLEASE STOP HANGING OUT WITH EZUMI!
?!

YOU'RE A FRIEND OF HIS?
OH...
TH-THE REASON HIS GRADES ARE DROPPING IS BECAUSE OF YOU...
HE'S NOT CUT OUT TO BE A TUTOR.
A-AND WHAT'S A GUY LIKE YOU GOING TO A UNIVERSITY FOR?
JOLT
WHAT THE HELL...
WHAT RIGHT DO YOU HAVE TO SAY THAT?
YOU WANNA FIGHT?! HUH?!
SHOCK
S-SO THIS IS HOW YOU THREATENED EZUMI INTO IT...
WHAT...?
AICH
TORAICHI

OTHER... OTHERWISE HE WOULDN'T DO SOME-THING LIKE THIS.
HE MUST'VE BEEN THREAT-ENED BY YOU...
ARE YOU *RETARD-ED?*
YOU THINK ANYONE CAN THREATEN THAT GUY?
THEN...
WHY WOULD HE GO AS FAR AS SACRIFICING HIMSELF FOR YOU?!
SACRI-FICING?
JUST RECENTLY, HE DROPPED TEN SPOTS IN THE CLASS RANKINGS.
FOR HIM NOT TO BE IN THE TOP THREE IS UNTHINK-ABLE.
...

I'VE BEEN COMPETING WITH HIM SINCE MIDDLE SCHOOL...
IF HE PULLS OUT NOW, IT'LL DESTROY MY PACE...
WHAT ABOUT **HIS** PACE...?
STEP
BUT WE BOTH WANT THIS, RIGHT?
RUSTLE
RUSTLE
CRAP... I THOUGHT I COULD SLEEP IN, TOO.
DAMN THIS MORNING!!
AND IT'S MY DAY OFF!!
SO IT'S MY FAULT, HUH?!
THUNK
CLATTER
CLATTER

IT PROBABLY IS...
IPPACHI?
IPPA-CHI!
HA
OH... SORRY.
WERE YOU ASLEEP?
NO!
I GUESS I SHOULD LET YOU GET SOME REAL REST DURING BREAKS, HUH?

YEAH, RIGHT...
BREAK'S THE ONLY FREE TIME WE HAVE.
...
I'M FINE...
AND YOU DON'T HAVE TO COME EVERY-DAY...
CLICK CLICK
I'D START TO FEEL RESPONSIBLE.
IT'S OKAY.
I JUST WANT TO SEE YOU.
WHA...
SLAP
DUMB-ASS! YOU'RE EMBAR RASSIN ME!
SLAP
GEEZ, YOU'RE TOO MUCH!
HA HA
TORAICHI
CUT THE CRAP!
BUT I'M SERIOUS.
...

EVEN WHEN I GO HOME, ALL I CAN THINK ABOUT IS YOU.

I WANT TO SEE YOU...EVERY SINGLE DAY...

MASA...

I LOVE YOU.

I CAN'T HANDLE IT WHEN I THINK ABOUT HOLDING YOU...

I... THIS IS THE FIRST I'VE FELT THIS WAY... AND IT SCARES ME, TOO.

MASASHI ...

OH...
NO...
I THINK I
SERIOUSLY
LIKE HIM...
TORAICHI
BUT...
IPPA-
CHI?
IT'LL BE
BAD.
SHOVE
AT THIS
RATE...
TORAICHI

MASA...

HAVE YOU BEEN THINKING THAT ALL ALONG?

SO YOU'RE JUST TOYING WITH ME WITH THAT KISS?!

THIS'S LIKE PROS-TITUTION.
WHAT... ?!
THEY SAY THOSE WHORES SELL THEIR BODIES, BU NOT THEIR LIPS...
I GUESS YOU'RE THE OPPO-SITE.
HOWEVER ...
THAT'S NOT MUCH OF A BARGAIN.
YOU'RE A GUY. YOU KNOW.

IT HAS TO BE SEX, RIGHT?
...
SUCK
SUCK HARDER. MAKE SOME NOISE.
SLURP
SUCK
SUCK
NN... MM...
RUB
DRIP
SUCK
YOU SEEM ALL INNOCENT, BUT YOU'VE GOT THE BALLS TO DO THAT.

YOU WANT TO CALL THIS SE
BETWEEN GUYS?
I'M SAYING ...
YOU'RE AFRAID OF ME COMING IN YOUR ASS, RIGHT?
SPLISH
TCH...
HA
HAA
RIDE ME.
FACE THIS WAY... SO I CAN SEE IT ALL.

AUGH...
STRAIN
STRAIN
TCH... AUGH...
HA
HAA
HA
YEAH... GOOD...
IT'S BEEN... TOO LONG...
HAA...
CREAK
SMACK
SQEAK
SMACK
WAY... TOO LONG...
CREAK
MA... MASASHI ...

DOES IT HURT?
IT'S BEEN SO LONG...
I DON'T REMEMBER WHAT FEELS GOOD FOR YOU.
THRUST
!
UGH ...
AH...
HA...
WAS IT HERE?
THRUST
AUGH...
THRUST
THRUST
AH!

OR HERE? OR WAS IT HERE?!
AH... I'M GONNA COME...
AH...!
HA
HA
SLAM
AH...
SLAM
JUST... SAY SOMETHING ...
QUIVER
AHH!
AHH!
JOLT
TREMBLE
SLAM
... TCH.
SQUEAK
WHY... HA...
WHY AREN'T YOU... RESISTING TODAY... AH.
CREAK
SQUEAK
TREMBLE
LIKE ALWAYS ...
CREAK
TREMBLE
WHY DON'T YOU... KICK ME OFF?
SQUEAK

STOP ME, DAMN IT...
IN THE END...
YOU MADE THE RIGHT CHOICE.

A FAREWELL FUCK... HUH.
OF COURSE...
AS IF HE WOULD SEE ME AGAIN.
I'M NOT A CHILD ANYMORE.
EZUMI!
SAITOU...
パァッ
SHINE
?
YOU FINALLY REMEMBER MY NAME!
I JUST WASN'T SPACING OUT FOR ONCE...
YOU DON'T HAVE TO CRY...
THANK GOODNESS... CHASING THAT GUY AWAY WAS THE RIGHT THING TO DO!
GUY...?

NO NEED TO THANK ME.
I KNOW EVERYTHING ABOUT YOU... THERE WAS A GUY BOTHERING YOU, RIGHT?
THE BRAINLESS GUY... HE'LL GIVE UP ON THE EXAMS SOON.
!!
YOU DID WHAT TO IPPACHI ?!
WHAT DID YOU SAY TO HIM?
I TOLD HIM ABOUT YOU, OF COURSE!
THAT EVERYTHING IS HIS FAULT...
NO WAY...
IPPACHI KNEW ABOUT IT...?
I'D START TO FEEL RESPONSIBLE.
SHIT... I WAS SO CONCEITED.
EZUMI?
NO...
THAT'S WHY HE BROKE IT OFF WITH ME?
IF HE WANTED TO BREAK UP WITH ME...
THAT WOULD'VE BEEN THE PERFECT
BUT...

WHY... DID HE HOLD ME LIKE THAT...?

HOLD YOU?

HUH?!

"A FAREWELL FUCK"?

NO.

YOU WOULDN'T HAVE COME UP WITH SOMETHING...

LIKE THAT.

WHAT DO YOU THINK OF ME?

I TOOK THE RISK OF TELLING HIM CLEARLY.

I CAN'T LEAVE YOU ALONE.

I HUNG ON TO THOSE WORDS.

I LIKE YOU.

I ONLY THOUGHT OF MY OWN FEELINGS.

love?
like?
WHY DO I REALIZE SOMETHING SO IMPORTANT...
NOW OF ALL TIMES?
EZUMI?!
EVEN IF IT'S FROM THE PAST.
I CAN'T GET OVER YOU IF I DON'T KNOW IT FIRST.
SINCE...
I STILL LIKE YOU...
MASHI?!

...?
IPPACHI, HE...
LOST HIS FOOTING AND...
DID YOU HEAR, IS THAT WHY YOU'RE HERE?!
?!
AH... WAIT!! PLEASE!
THE OPERATION IS STILL IN PROGRESS!
手術中
OPERATION IN PROGRESS
KAZUYA... KAZUYA'S IN THERE, RIGHT?!
SLAM
SLAM
ARE YOU A FRIEND OF THE PATIENT?
IF YOU ARE...
KAZUYA!
PLEASE CALM DOWN...

MASA... SHI?
KA...
KAZUY-...
WAH!
WOW...
MA-MASASHI...
HEY!
WHY ARE YOU HERE...
OH? IPPACHI'S TEACHER!

LISTEN TO THIS!
THE BASTARD FELL FROM THE SECOND FLOOR AND ONLY SPRAINED HIS ANKLE!
THE WAY HE DIDN'T MOVE, I THOUGHT HE WAS DEAD! THEN HE SUDDENLY JUMPED UP IN THE AMBULANCE.
WHAT DO YOU THINK HE SAID?!
STO-
STOP IT!
?
GAH HA HA
IT'S ALL TRUE!
WELL, EXCUSE ME!
SLAP
SLAP
"MASASHI♡, I'M SORRY♡!"
DON'T SAY IT LIKE *THAT*, UGH!
SO...
IN THE END, HE WAS JUST ASLEEP.
WORRYING US FOR NOTH-ING!
NO...
IT'S UM...
CAN I TAKE HIM HOME?
?
...
I'LL KILL YOU!

AH!
HEY! WHAT ABOUT THE MEDICAL BILLS?!
HEY, MASA ...
MASASHI ...?!
WHY DID YOU APOLOGIZE TO ME?
!!
STUPID... I WAS TALKING IN MY SLEEP.
WHAT WERE YOU DREAMING OF?
WAS I DOING SOMETHING BAD YOU?
NO!
NO... THAT'S NOT IT.
I WAS WRONG.
WHY?!

IT'S ONLY NATURAL THAT YOU WERE MAD.
... WHAT?
I NEVER TOLD YOU HOW I FELT.
NOT ONCE...
I DECEIVED YOU...
I... I'VE NEVER FALLEN IN LOVE BEFORE.
I'VE NEVER LIKED SOMEONE SO MUCH, EITHER...

I WAS SCARED ...
I USED THE EXCUSE...
THAT I DID IT FOR YOU.
BUT I WAS REALLY JUST AFRAID OF GOING ANY FURTHER.
BUT...
I STILL WANT YOU AFTER ALL...

OH... SO YOU'RE JUST LIKE ME.
RIGHT?
...SO DON'T GO WORRYING BY YOUR-SELF ANYMORE.
HMPH
KISS
YOU'RE SO SIMPLE-MINDED.
YOU'LL EXPLODE.
YOU'RE SHAME-LESS.
HA HA
KA-
KAZUYA ...?!
DRIP
HM.
YOU'RE FAIRLY SIM-PLEMINDED YOURSELF, HERE.
GULP

I LOVE YOU...
PLEASE...
HAA ...
NEVER STOP TELLING ME.
じーっ
STARE
IPPACHI...
MY... DICK?
NO!
WHO ARE YOU HOLDING?!
EZUMI!
HOLD MEEE!
WHISPER WHISPER
...
SHAMELESS.
生意気。2 / TELL ME YOU'RE IN LOVE
end

# BREAK TIME THREEWAY

## MASAMUNE SAITOU (AGE 17) ROUGH AFTERNOON

IS IT... TOO TIGHT? SAITOU...

NO... IT'S GOOD.

HA

E–
EZUMI ...!
TCH ...
I'M ...
GONNA COME ...
AHH...
EZUMI... WAKE HIM UP.
AND HE'S THE TOP, TOO.
TREMBLE
TREMBLE
AH...
END.

HEY... I CAN'T CHANGE YOUR MIND?
NO.
ONE DAY WITH THE LOVEBIRDS. 1
...
GUH!
BASTARD !!
PINCH
DAMN IT!! YOU GOT ME OUT!
BUT YOU TOLD ME VIDEO GAMES BORED YOU.
YOU WERE THE ONE THAT BROUGHT IT HERE!
WANNA ... DO IT?
NO.
INSTANT ANSWER
YOU'RE BEING A WEIRD ASSHOLE.
PERVERT
...

THEN... GIVE ME A TOWEL
HUH?
ONE YOU'VE USED TODAY.
A TOWEL... WHAT FOR?
BLOW
YOUR BOXERS WOULD WORK, TOO.
NICE AND WARM.
BOXERS...
AAAAH!
MY TOWEL...
THE REASON THEY GO MISSING IS YOU?!
OF COURSE!!
HOW MUCH DO YOU THINK THEY COST?!
...ABOUT 100 YEN FOR FIVE?
I CAN GIVE THEM BACK, BUT...
THEY MIGHT BE STUCK TOGETHER...
A GLANCE!!
SPURT
HEEL DROP
I DON'T WANT 'EM!!
STAY AWAY, PERV!
END.

...GRADUATION ALBUM?
MINE?
SLURP SLURP

# ONE DAY WITH THE LOVEBIRDS. 2

WHY WOULD YOU WANT TO LOOK AT THAT?
I SWEAR I WON'T USE IT FOR ANYTHING WEIRD.
OF COURSE NOT!
I PROBABLY LEFT SOMETHING LIKE THAT AT MY PARENTS' HOUSE.
NO. IT'S PROBABLY IN YOUR CLOSET.
I WONDER...
SMIRK

AH...
JUST
FORGET
IT.
I JUST
ASKED ON
A WHIM.
NO! I HAVE
A FEELING IT'S
SOMEWHERE
AROUND HERE.
STUBBORN PERSONALITY.
WHAT
ABOUT
THAT BOX
THERE?
LOOKS LIKE
IT COULD BE
IN IT.
OH! I HAVEN'T
EVEN UNPACKED
THAT BOX...
HM?
CLICK
PITCH DARK
MASA...
SHOCK
PUFF
PUFF
I'VE ALWAYS
WANTED TO
TRY IT IN THE
CLOSET...
BASTARD
...
NN...
WOW...
IT ECHOES...
SO HOT...
TWITCH
HAA...
NN.
KISS
NEXT DOOR.
NN!
BANG
SLURP
I'M
GONNA
FAIL
FOR THE
THIRD
TIME...
TOKYO UNI!
THEY
SOUND
EVEN
CLOSER
TODAY...
SIGH
CLATTER
CLATTER
CLATTER
AH!
TCH...
SLICK
MM!
BANG
BANG
END.
BREAK TIME end

I'M NOT YOUR
「生意気っ子」
STEPPIN' STONE
SHAMELESS
HERE.
IT'S NOT "A". IT'S "E".
YOU SPELLED A LOT OF WORDS WRONG HERE.
PAY ATTENTION OR IT'LL COST YOU.
THIS GUY, MASASHI EZUMI.
CURRENTLY ATTENDING AN ELITE UNIVERSITY PREP SCHOOL (AGE 17, SECOND YEAR IN HIGH SCHOOL).
GEEZ... AND YOU MANAGE TO DO WELL ON THE OTHER PARTS.
WHAT IF YOU LOSE POINTS WITH THIS?
I'M KAZUYA SAKAI (AGE 23, A SCAFFOLD CONSTRUCTOR).
HE'S MY TUTOR.

I'M NOT YOUR
「生意気。3」
STEPPIN' STONE
LOVELY
AND WE'RE LOVERS.

I'VE WORKED HARD FOR OVER A YEAR NOW AND THE TIME I HAVE UNTIL THE EXAM IS...
ONE MORE WEEK.
ALSO, THE PLURAL ...
WHAT DO YOU MEAN "CHILDS"?
IT'S "CHILDREN"!
THIS IS SO BASIC!
YOU CAN'T JUST USE AN "S" HERE.
IT DOESN'T MATTER HOW SMALL THE MISTAKE IS ON THE EXAMS.
THERE ARE NO PITY POINTS.
WHAT IS IT...
THAT I...
LIKE ABOUT HIM?
AND NO MATTER WHAT, THOSE ARE PECS.
PECS AND A MEAN LOOK.
PFFT.
WHAT I LIKE IS MORE LIKE THIS...
PLUMP...
SUPER-SOFT...

LIKE MARSH-MALLOWS...
ARE YOU LISTENING?
BA-
BUMP
RAZOR SHARP GLARE
WHA-
...
WHAT? OF COURSE I GET IT. UH, THE "A'S" AND "E'S".
THEN THE PLU-RALS.
IT'S NOT MY PROBLEM IF YOU GET POINTS DEDUCTED FOR IT.
HE SCARED ME...
PANT PANT PANT
DID YOU MAKE A WORD BOOK?
WRITE DOWN ONES YOU HAVE TROUBLE WITH.
WELL...

I GUESS HE'S PRETTY NICE IN OTHER WAYS.
SURE. SHOULD I MAKE SOME TEA BEFORE WE START MATH?
HE'S SHAMELESS.
AND STUBBORN.
IN OTHER WORDS, RATHER THAN TASTE...
...
?!
THERE'S THE FACT THAT HE'S A GUY.
MA...
MASASHI-KUN?

YOU ... FEEL LIKE DOING IT, DON'T YOU?
?!
NO... I DON'T ...
LIAR... YOU'VE BEEN OGLING ME THIS WHOLE TIME.
BASTARD ...
DON'T SAY THAT LIKE SOME VIOLATED OLD LADY ON A BUS...
PUFF
SHALL WE TAKE A LOOK?
I WONDER.
PULL
GUH?!
LOOK ...

AREN'T YOU THE LEAST BIT HARD?
NO...
YOU...
SAY, IPPACHI ...
PUSH
YOU DON'T HAVE A LOT OF HAIR.
SLIP
STOP IT.
DAMN!
AND THE COLOR...
IT REALLY STANDS OUT.
BLUSH
HAA
WOW...
YOU'RE GETTING REALLY HARD...
THIS...
HAA
HAA
PERVERTED BASTARD...

WANT MORE OF THIS?
I TAKE IT ALL BACK!
THERE'S NOTHING NICE ABOUT HIM!
HAA...
HA
QUIVER
QUIVER
HA...
TREMBLE
HAA...
HA
HA
SLIP
HA ...
POP
HAA
SHIT.
WE WENT ALL THE WAY IN THE END...
THREE TIMES, TO BOOT.
I'M FUCKING EXHAUSTED ...

AND I ONLY HAVE ONE WEEK LEFT!
...SO?
YOU STARTED IT...
SHOVE
I WAS FIGHTING THE URGE FOR SO LONG, TOO.
BULL-SHIT!!
WE JUST DID IT TWO DAYS AGO!
I HAD TO WAIT ONE WHOLE DAY!
HOW MANY TIMES DO YOU THINK I JERKED OFF?
FLUSH
JERKED OFF...
HOW THE HELL SHOULD I KNOW?!
NO MORE!
A-ANYWAY, THAT'S IT!

NEVER AGAIN UNTIL I FINISH THE EXAMS!!
IF YOU CAN'T HANDLE IT, DON'T BOTHER COMING HERE!
...GET IT?
HEY!!
...
HUH?
HE'S QUIET.
CAN YOU STAND IT...?
SO, YOU'RE OKAY...
WITH NOT SEEING ME?
MASASHI?
YOU SAID UNTIL AFTER THE TEST...
FOR REAL...

SO AFTER YOU PASS, WHEN WILL WE MEET AGAIN?
YOU WORK DURING THE DAY AND ATTEND SCHOOL AT NIGHT.
HUH...?
WHEN DO YOU PLAN TO SEE ME?
OH...
OH... COME ON!
YOU'RE GONNA WORRY ABOUT THAT?
LET'S SEE IF I PASS FIRST...
HA HA
DON'T TAKE THE TEST.

YOU DON'T LOOK LIKE YOU'RE INTO IT ANYWAY.
AND WHAT'S GOING TO CHANGE?
YOU DON'T PLAN ON CHANGING JOBS, SO JUST FORGET ABOUT IT.
...
NOWADAYS EDUCATIONAL BACKGROUNDS ...
SHUT UP.
DON'T EVEN SAY IT.
SHOCK

DESPITE MAKING FUN OF ME.
WHO DO YOU THINK PUT THIS IN MY HEAD?
COMING FROM A PRESTIGIOUS STUDENT LIKE YOU? DON'T PATRONIZE ME.
ARE YOU A COLLEGE DROPOUT?
I WASN'T MAKING FUN...
THAT WAS JUST...
I JUST WANTED TO PUT YOU OFF...
I DON'T CARE!
I KNOW THAT ALREADY.
STILL...
I'M TAKING THE TEST.
I DON'T CARE IF IT'S RECKLESS. I STARTED SO I HAVE NO INTENTION OF QUITTING.
THE THING THAT'LL BOTHER ME LATER IS...

I'LL KEEP FALLING DEEPER FOR YOU.
WHAT ...
AND I'D WANT TO BE CLOSER TO YOU ...
SO THAT MEANS YOU'RE JUST DOING THIS TO MAKE YOURSELF BETTER THAN THE REST?
I SEE HOW IT IS!
THEN YOU CAN DO WHATEVER THE HELL YOU WANT ALONE!
AND STILL...
LIKE YOU'D PASS ANYWAY!
THE FUCK YOU SAY...

BA-BUMP
AH. TEARS?!
THAT'S WHY.
MASASHI!
DO YOU STILL NOT GET IT?
RUNNING OFF LIKE THAT, WE'RE ACTING LIKE GIRLS...
HM?
SLIP
IS IT JUST ME?

GUH!
THIS IS MY APPLICATION!
TISSUE!
TISSUE!
↑ WELL-AIMED...
WHO SAID IT WOULDN'T BE LONELY?
BLEH ...
SIGH
SERIOUSLY.
WE SHOULD BE TOGETHER.
CAN I...?
WHA...

NO ...
WAIT...
HAA ...
HA
KAZUYA...
TCH...
KAZUYA ...
LOVE YOU...
I LOVE YOU...
KAZUYA.

SLIDE
JOLT
I HEARD YOU WERE TAKING THE EXAMS.
GUH
WHOA WHOA!
WHOOPS.
BUT TO GET SOMETHING LIKE THIS...
I GUESS YOU HAVE FREE TIME?
RUB RUB
UWAAH!
?!

CHANGE YOUR TASTE IN WOMEN?
SHE'S GOT TO BE A CRAZY BITCH.
BITE MARKS! ♥
KOUSEI?!
LONG TIME NO SEE.
WHAT'S UP?
WHY'RE YOU HERE?
WHAT A GREETING...
I'M SAD...
I HEARD THEY WERE HIRING, SO HERE I AM.
I CLUNG TO THE BOSS IN TEARS TO GET THIS JOB.
HM...
WHAT?
I THOUGHT THINGS WERE GOING WELL.
THIS GUY...
HE'S KOUSEI MOGI, AGE 23.

HE WAS A FORMER CONSTRUCTION BUDDY WHO WENT SOLO A YEAR AGO.
RIGHT NOW, THE GUYS AND I ARE WORKING ON THE PROJECT HE LEFT BEHIND.
THE REASON WAS...
THIS GUY FROM NAGANO MESSED UP.
HE INJURED A KID FROM THE NEIGHBORHOOD...
SERIOUSLY?
WELL, THE INJURY ITSELF WAS MINOR.
BUT BUSINESS SLOWED DOWN DRASTICALLY.
I HAD TO LAY THE GUY OFF.
WHAT A PAIN.
WOW, THAT'S AWFUL...
HEY.
WHY ARE YOU TAKING THE EXAMS ANYWAY?
UH.
BA-BUMP

I DON'T LIKE IT.
IS THERE ANY WAY TO CHANGE YOUR MIND?
WE MAKE SUCH A GOOD TEAM.
IF YOU START EARLY, YOU COULD EVEN HAVE YOUR OWN COMPANY ONE DAY. WHAT DO YOU THINK?
YEAH...
I'VE THOUGHT ABOUT THAT BEFORE, BUT...
YOU'RE BEING VAGUE...
THAT'S UNLIKE YOU.
ARE YOU CAUGHT UP WITH A BAD CHICK?
POKE
THUMP
DON'T TELL ME SHE'S THE ONE *MAKING* YOU DO IT.
THUMP
YOU ...
THAT'S NONE OF YOUR BUSINESS!
SO I WAS RIGHT.
YOU'RE TOO EASY.

WELL, THAT'S WHAT I LIKE ABOUT YOU.
YOUR SIMPLICITY.
I'M NOT SIMPLE ...
THAT'S WHY IT'S SUCH A PAIN.
OH? MASHI DIDN'T COME TODAY.
GOOD WORK!
YEAH!
BA-BUMP
WHO'S MASHI
IPPACHI'S TUTOR.
A STUDENT FROM THAT SCHOOL NEAR HERE.
ALWAYS PICKING HIM UP.
NOT ANYMORE.
IT'S SELF-STUDY THIS WEEK.
OHO. SO YOU OVER-IMPOSED, HUH?
THEN, YOU'RE GONNA FAIL?
HA HA!
SHUT UP!
...

IS MASHI A GIRL?
HUH?
OF COURSE NOT!
EVEN I'D GO FOR THE TEST IF IT BAGGED ME SUCH A SWEET DEAL.
THAT'S ENOUGH ...
KOUSEI, YOU HAVE A MOTORBIKE, RIGHT?
LET'S RIDE IT!
LET'S DRINK!
YAY...
WAH!
HOLD ON!
?

DON'T PUT THEM ON MY BOOKS!
THEY'LL GET WET!
HUH?
FORGET ABOUT THEM TODAY.
YOU KNOW ...
I HAVE LESS THAN A WEEK TO STUDY!
YOU HAVE TO LEAVE AFTER THAT DRINK.
GEEZ, YOU BOUGHT SO MANY...
JUST SIT DOWN!
SO?
HOW YOU DOING WITH THE GIRL?
I TOLD YOU ...
QUIT BUGGING ME!
I'M WORRIED. YOU DON'T SEEM TO BE HANDLING EVERYTHING VERY WELL.
AND YOU SEEM TO BE HAVING ISSUES WITH THE GIRL.
...

HEH HEH.
IS SHE CHUBBY? HM?
THE HELL?
YOU LIKE THEM, RIGHT? THOSE UGLY FAT CHICKS.
THAT'S ALL YOU DATED BACK THEN.
DON'T CALL THEM THAT!
BA-BUMP
BUT THIS ONE'S DIFFER-ENT.
FEELS ALMOST... DANGER-OUS.
SHE MUST BE AN OLDER WOMAN, OR A PRO.
NOPE. YOU'D NEVER GUESS.
POINT
OH, REALLY?
EITHER WAY, YOU'RE HAVING GOOD SEX, AREN'T YOU?
YOU LOOK LIKE YOU GOT LAID.
GOT LAID...
WHA.

HMM...
KIND OF LIKE A GIRL AFTE POPPING HE CHERRY.
I GUESS?
WHY DO YOU SAY GIRL?!
HEY!
WELL, YOU'RE NOT WILD ABOUT SEX, RIGHT?
I FIGURED.
IT'S ...
NOT LIKE I DON'T LIKE IT!
DAMNED PERVERT!
YOU...
WHEN YOU HAVE FUN IN A RELATIONSHIP YOU USUALLY WON'T SHUT U ABOUT IT.
THEN YOU MAKE AN ASS OUT OF YOURSELF AFTER SEX, AM I RIGHT?
...

BUT IT'S DIFFERENT THIS TIME.
YOU WANT THIS, BUT IT'S HARD ON YOU.
THAT'S WHAT I SEE.
STOP...
DAMN...
ARE YOU DRUNK?
THIS GUY...
DID HE DRINK THAT MUCH?
I WONDER...
I'M NOT DOING ANYTHING OUT OF THE ORDINARY.
WHEN...
I SAW THIS...
JOLT

IT DROVE ME CRAZY.
GRAB
KOUSEI ?!
WHAT'S SO GOOD ABOUT HER, HUH?
THE COCK SUCKING? THE TIT FUCKING?
SHIFT
WAIT...
YOU'VE PROBABLY NEVER HAD A CHICK UNDER YOU, HUH?
HEH HEH
BAS-TARD ...
WHAT'S WRONG WITH YOU?
DON'T TELL ME SHE DID YOU IN THE ASS, TOO...
LET'S SEE!
?!
WAH!
WHAT'S THIS?
じに
SQUEEZE
じに
SQUEEZE
HAA... NN!
JOLT
SHOCK

SHIT...
WAS THAT ME?
HOW DID IT GET LIKE THIS...
AH !
?!

SINCE WHEN ?
MASA ...
"MASHI" ?
AH...
THIS...

ISN'T WHAT IT LOOKS LIKE?
HE'S A FRIEND.
HE'S JUST A LITTLE DRUNK.
WHAT'S... UP?
I THOUGHT YOU WEREN'T COMING...
YOU THOUGHT I WASN'T COMING...
SO YOU USED THE CHANCE TO...?
MASA...
HEH
HM...
STUDYING HARD, I SEE.
NO NEED FOR A TUTOR WHEN YOU'VE GOT BOOZE AND ASS, HUH?
!!

I'M OF NO USE.
MASASHI...
WAIT...
AH...
GRIP
STUDY CARDS?
THAT'S...
JERK
!
HUH?

MASASHI.
SLAM
WHAT...
A MESS.
NO WAY...
SPEECHLESS
HE WAS CRYING?
OVER SOMETHING LIKE THIS?
IS IT MY FAULT?
AH
SNORE
SNORT
WHY ME?
THIS GUY...

...
I'VE NEVER EVEN MADE A GIRL CRY.
受付
THERE WAS NEVER A PROBLEM.
校内最徐行
BUT THE TRUTH IS...
I NEVER HAD TO THINK ABOUT IT.
I WANTED A PICTURE PERFECT LOVE.
SO I ALWAYS WENT FOR THE NICE GIRLS.

REFRESHING CONVERSATIONS...
CASUAL SEX...
USED TO ME ALREADY?
YOU'RE REALLY TAKING ME IN...
SHIT... I'M GONNA...
COME SO HARD...
KAZUYA...
I'M COMING INSIDE...

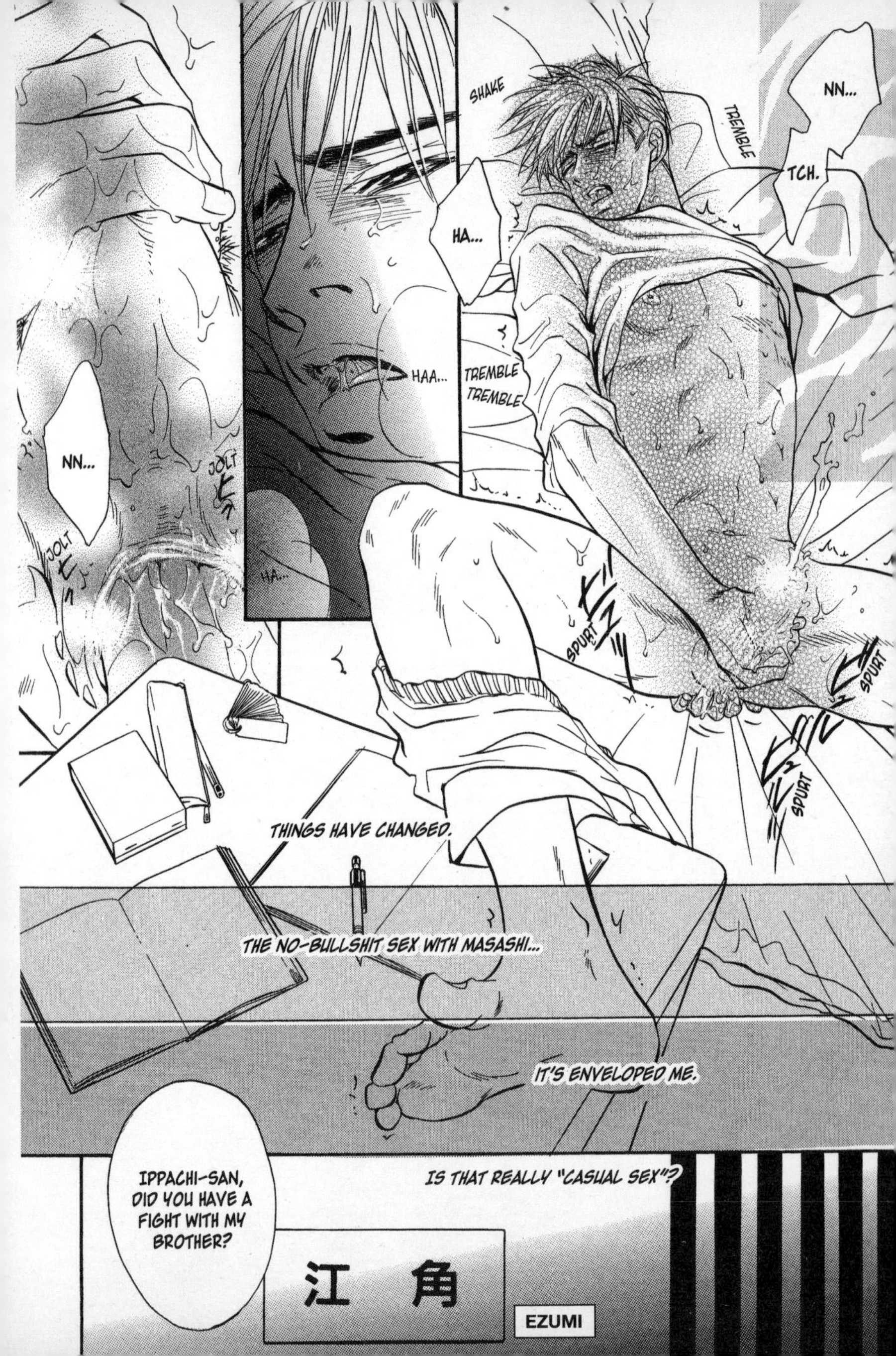
NN...
TREMBLE
TCH.
SHAKE
HA...
TREMBLE
TREMBLE
SPURT
SPURT
SPURT
HAA...
HA...
NN...
JOLT
JOLT
THINGS HAVE CHANGED.
THE NO-BULLSHIT SEX WITH MASASHI...
IT'S ENVELOPED ME.
IS THAT REALLY "CASUAL SEX"?
IPPACHI-SAN, DID YOU HAVE A FIGHT WITH MY BROTHER?
江角
EZUMI

AT A TIME LIKE THIS... I'M SORRY!
EHEH. JUST...
UM...
JUST FIGURED I'D LET YOU KNOW WHAT'S UP.
CUTE AS ALWAYS, NACCHAN...
MY STUPID BROTHER...
WHY DON'T YOU COME INSIDE AND CLEAR THE AIR WITH HIM?!
NO. NO THANKS.
JUST LETTING YOU KNOW THAT I'M TAKING THE TEST TOMORROW.
AN ANGEL...
YEAH!
DO YOUR BEST!
FIGHT!!
WHAT SHOULD I DO?
I DIDN'T STUDY AT ALL THIS WEEK.
I'M DEAD.
EVERY TIME I OPENED THE BOOK...
I'D SEE HIS FACE.
THE PAIN. THE HEAT.
?!

RUSTLE
MASASHI ?!
HEY...
WE EVEN DID IT HERE...
...
!!
IT WAS MY FIRST TIME AND I WAS TOO INTO IT.
THAT WAS WHY I DID IT.

WHAT... ARE YOU SAYING?
I ONLY WANTED TO FUCK YOU.
CRASH
TCH...
I'M DOING IT.
IT'S BEEN TOO LONG.
BASTARD...
WHEN ARE YOU GONNA QUIT ACTING LIKE A KID?
IF IT'S ABOUT THE GUY FROM BEFORE...
DAMN YOUR EXCUSES.

FUN, ISN'T IT?
YOUR LITTLE SUPERIORITY GAME.
GAME?
I KNOW YOU'RE CAPABLE OF THAT.
I REALIZE THAT IT DOESN'T MATTER WHO IT IS.
YOUR VALUES AND SEX...
DO YOU GET OFF ON GETTING BETTER PEOPLE?
BASTARD ...
GIVE ME A FUCKING BREAK.
THEN LET'S BREAK UP.
FOR REAL, THIS TIME.
?!

YOU'RE TOO NAIVE.
I END UP TAKING ADVANTAGE OF YOU.
AREN'T YOU EMBARRASSED BY A WHINING BRAT LIKE ME?
YOU **ARE** "THE MAN" IPPACHI-SAN.
YEAH, I'M EMBAR-RASSED.

I CAN'T STUDY WITH MY ASS BOTHERING ME.
I CAN'T TAKE THE TEST LIKE THIS.
IT'S LIKE I'M GOING THROUGH PUBERTY AGAIN. YOU MAKE MY HEAD AND DICK ACHE.
KAZUYA ?!
YOU'RE RESPONSI-BLE.

KA...
WHAT? HURRY UP AND STRIP...
KAZUYA... SERIOUSLY?
ISN'T ...
THE TEST TOMORROW?
SHUT UP.
RUSTLE
YOU WERE ALL READY AT FIRST, WEREN'T YOU?
SAID SOME PRETTY SHAMELESS THINGS, TOO.
PERVERTED FREAK.
FLICK
JOLT
PERVERTED ...

I GET IN THE MOOD, TOO.
TWITCH
DON'T TREAT ME LIKE A GIRL.
HA...
NN...
TWITCH
KAZ...
TREMBLE
MASASHI...
HA...
I CAN'T GET ENOUGH OF THIS...
YOUR EROTIC EXPRESSIONS...
TREMBLE

TELL ME...
HAA
HA
I WANT IT ALL THE TIME.
WHAT DO YOU WANT?
HA
HAA... HA
TREMBLE
DRIP
HAA... IN...
INSIDE.
NOPE.
AH!
SQUEEZE
PLEASE... LET ME...
THIS IS THE ONLY TIME YOU LISTEN TO ME...
SLIP
MASASHI.
DRIP
NIBBLE
YOU'RE SO BAD... I SHOULD PUNISH YOU.
YOU'RE TOO DEFIANT.
HAA
NN!
AH!
HA...
PUSHY...

SELF-CENTERED...
ILL-TEMPERED...
HA...?!
KAZUYA ?!
AH!
SLIP
GAH!
AHH!
RUB
RUB
...?
SPLASH
SPURT
SPURT
SPLASH
!
TCH...
ABUSIVE...
SPURT

ADORABLE.
THAT WAS QUICK.
BLUSH
YOU LOVE ME THAT MUCH?
I...
TODAY I...
BECAUSE HE...
THAT YOU'D CRY BECAUSE OF ME?
HAA...
HA...
HAA...
...

I LOVE YOU...
AND I'LL ALWAYS FEEL THAT WAY.
START... MOVING...
HA
THE BAD GUY...
IS ME.
I CAN'T EXPRESS THINGS VERY WELL VERBALLY.
AH...
SO I'LL USE MY THOUGHTS.
AH!
HAA...
NGH...
CREAK
YOU'RE SPECIAL TO ME.
CREAK
HA...
AH

MASASHI ...
MASA... SHI.
THE TEST, MY PRIDE ...
HAA
HA
I COULD THROW THEM ALL AWAY FOR YOU.
HA
MASASHI...
TCH...
MASASHI ...
THRUST
SLIP
MASASHI...
SLIDE
HA
AH... AH!
KAZUYA...
TREMBLE
KAZUYA...
HA
HAA
I'M GONNA...
HA
DO IT...
SPLSH
LET ME SEE YOU...
ME TOO...
SPLSH
SQUISH
SLISH
THIS IS HOW MUCH ...
AH...
OH...

I'VE FALLEN IN LOVE WITH YOU.
SPURT
SPURT
SPURT
PANT
PANT
MASHI?
WHAT ABOUT SCHOOL?
IS IPPACHI HERE?
OVER THERE
CAN YOU DO SOMETHING ABOUT HIM?
GLOOM
SOB SOB
FAILED. FAIL-ING. FAILURE. TO FAIL.
FAIL...
WORD CONJUGATION
SOB SOB SOB
IPPACHI!

YOU...
PASSED THE TEST.
?!
SERIOUSLY?!
YES.
WELL, SINCE I TUTORED YOU, IT'S ONLY TO BE EXPECTED.
...
IN THE END...
YOU SAID I'D FAIL...
I WENT AND TOOK THE TEST.
AFTER HAVING SEX TILL DAWN...
WHOO!
YOU DID IT! YOU CAN GO TO SCHOOL!
AH!
FLAMES
IT'S HIM!
...
I'M NOT GOING.
WHAT?!

I NEVER REALLY PLANNED ON GOING BACK.
IPPACHI?
I JUST WANTED TO SHOW YOU THAT I CAN.
HEH.
HUH?
SO WHAT DO YOU THINK OF THIS MANLY DEED? → ?
I HAD TO DO IT.
IT... WAS FOR ME?!
TURN
YOU IDIOT.
USING UP MY TIME LIKE THAT...
AH.
DOES THIS MEAN... WE GET TO DO IT EVERY DAY?
YOU GET A FEW DAYS!
BASTARD!
SICK LOVE-BIRDS.
...
OH, LOVE.
#2
UNEQUALED #1
LATER FOR KOUSEI.
HEY... WHO'S "KAZUYA"?
SHOCK
GOO GOO
HE IS A MARRIED MAN.
SHAMELESS 3 / LOVELY — end

# マシュマロハネムーン
# MARSHMALLOW HONEYMOON

HEY... NACCHI'S BROTHER HAS A GOOD FUTURE AHEAD OF HIM,
DON'T YOU THINK?
ARE YOU REALLY BLOOD RELATED?
YOU KNOW...
IF HE WAS MY BROTHER...

I'D WAKE HIM UP EVERY MORNING.
SIGH ♥
YOU'RE THE ONE WHO'S DREAMING RIGHT NOW.
AH HA HA
JUST WISHING HE WAS MY BROTHER INSTEAD.
WOULDN'T THAT JUST COMPLICATE THINGS?
HOW'S IT GOING?
NOT TO MENTION HE GOES TO A GREAT SCHOOL!
...
YOU CAN TELL THE DIFFERENCE BETWEEN HIM AND THE AVERAGE GUY! ♡
SQUEE
STUPID, HE CAN HEAR!
LOOK, LOOK! HE'S DISTRESSED!!
HE LOOKS SO SMART!!
SQUEE
...

MASASHI EZUMI, AGE 18 (HIGH SCHOOL SENIOR)
I'M SO HORNY...
SIGH
SQUEAL!
HE SIGHED! ♡
HE CAN HEAR YOU...
DISTRESSED
I HATE SUMMER BREAK.
TRAVEL?
SUMMER'S IMPOSSIBLE FOR ME.
CAN'T YOU TAKE A SMALL BREAK?
NOPE.
BECAUSE SOMEONE WANTS TO HAVE THE LUXURY OF AN AIR CONDITIONER AT MY PLACE.
SO I HAVE TO WORK.
MY LOVER...

BUILDS SCAFFOLDS.
BESIDES, TRAVELING WITH YOU IS KINDA...
KAZUYA SAKAI, AGE 24 (SCAFFOLD CONSTRUCTOR)
WHAT?
NO DOUBT WHAT'S GOING ON IN YOUR MIND.
CRAMPED IN AN INN TOGETHER.
BULL'S EYE
!!
THAT'S NOT TRUE!!
OH? CAN YOU STAND NOT GETTING ANY FOR A WEEK?
IF YOU CAN, I'LL GO.
SO CRUEL.
I CAN!!
OKAY THEN.
THEN DON'T LAY A SINGLE FINGER ON ME FOR A WHOLE WEEK.
A FINGER ...
SOB
TWO FINGERS.
WILD DELUSIONS
HE'S SO DEEP IN THOUGHT!
TOTALLY INTO IT!

HUH?
WHERE ARE YOU GOING?
IPPA-CHI'S PLACE.
MOM'S GOING TO BE MAD IF YOU DON'T MAKE IT BACK FOR DINNER.
I KNOW.
YOU SHOULDN'T BOTHER IPPACHI-SAN SO MUCH, EITHER.
SHUT UP!
SO TALL
SUCH LONG LEGS!
IF ONLY HIS PERSONALITY WAS BETTER...
SIGH
SORRY HE'S SO RUDE.
SIGH ...
I WONDER IF HE HAS A GIRLFRIEND ...
NACC
I WANT TO GO OUT WITH HIM!
CAN I?!
HUH?
NOTHING I CAN DO.
BUT MIYUKI, WHAT ABOUT TOORU?
※ POSER
TOORU
MIYUKI, LOVE!
UGLY
GROSS
NOT EVEN!
HE'S NOT MY BOY-FRIEND.
THAT P.U.G.

THE THING IS...
I'M WEAK FOR THE COOL, GLASSES TYPE.
YOU'RE IN LOVE, HUH?
I'M IN LOVE!
GOOD WORK!
YEAH, YOU TOO!
HEY! MASHI, LONG TIME NO SEE!
BA-BUMP
IS YOUR PREP SCHOOL NEARBY?
YOU EVEN KNOW OUR NEW SITE!
MASASHI?
NO, I'M NOT GOING TO PREP SCHOOL.
BUT YOU'RE A SENIOR.
WHAT ABOUT EXAMS?
IT'S NOT REALLY A BIG DEAL.
WHAT, NOT TRYING FOR TOKYO UNIVER-SITY?!

GEEZ...
LIKE WE COULD TELL WHAT HE'S THINKING WITH A FACE LIKE THAT.
OH.
YOU TWO...
STILL SCREWING?
...
WH-
WHAT, SO?
HE'S GONNA ROT YOUR BRAINS, MASHI!
RUSTLE
RUSTLE
WHAT THE HELL?
GAH HA HA
YOU'LL CATCH HIS STUPIDITY!
MASASHI.
HEY!

HEY...
AREN'T YOU LETTING ME ON?
WE'RE WALKING?
IF YOU RIDE... I'LL TOUCH YOU.
UH?!
CLINGING ONTO ME LIKE THAT...
!!
IDIOT...
ACTING LIKE A BRAT AGAIN.
WHAT? YOU SAID SO...
YEAH, BUT...
YOU KNOW WHAT I MEAN.
FORGET TRAVEL-ING ...

YOU ...
CALLED ME A BEAST BEFORE.
SO I WANTED TO SHOW YOU ANOTHER SIDE OF ME.
MASASHI ...
PANG
AH!
GAH!
AH!
MA...
MASASHI!

SPURT
SPURT
AH ...!
SHOCK
JOLT
JOLT
HA
HA
AH!
TWITCH
HAA
HAA...
NO MATTER HOW MUCH I COME, I'M STILL HARD...
IT FEELS SO GOOD WHEN YOU'RE FULL OF MY CUM...
CREAK
HA

HA
CREAK
YOU LIKE IT WHEN I KEEP IT INSIDE AND RAM YOU...
CAN YOU TAKE IT?
CREAK
HA
LOOK...
SQUEAK
YOU... BASTARD.
I'M IN SO DEEP.
AHH!
CREAK
SQUEAK
HA
CREAK
TREMBLE
AH... WOW... I'M GETTING SUCKED IN...
HA
HA
KAZUYA...
YOU'RE COMING ...
ME TOO...
JOLT
JOLT
JOLT
TCH...
SLAM
SLAM
SLAM
...

YOU MONSTER.
SCOPPIE
UH.
YOU...
HAVE NO OTHER SIDE.
YOU GOT BACK FIVE DAYS' WORTH...
BUT YOU ENJOYED IT, TOO...
SHUT UP.
THAT WAS JUST TURGID WOOD.
WHAT DOES THAT MEAN?
BLUSH
NO.
NOTHING YOU UNDERAGED KIDS NEED TO KNOW!!
HMPH.
THERE IS SOMETHING HE DOESN'T KNOW.
TURGID WOOD... WHEN ONE IS EXTREMELY EXHAUSTED BUT STILL MANAGES TO BE ERECT. A MYSTERIOU PHENOMENON (DURING SEX).

FINE, I'LL JUST ASK NATSUKO.
NO!
アワ
アワ
YOU STUPID BASTARD!
I'LL ASK MY MOM.
YOU FUCKING KNOW.
DON'T.
THIS!!
THAT'S CHEAP! I ASKED YOU!
SMACK
DAMN... IF YOU WANNA KNOW SO BADLY, LOOK IT UP.
ALL YOU READ ARE TEXTBOOKS.
?
YOU WANTED TO KNOW.
Bábi
A BIG BOY'S HYPER MAGAZINE. OUR SEX. RIM JOBS! BUTT SEX!
YOU KNOW ...
YOU SHOULDN'T LET NACCHAN OR YOUR MOM FIND THAT.
KEEP QUIET ABOUT IT.
SIGH
...
I'M SURPRISED.
FIRST TIME SEEING SUCH A THING.

PSSH ...
FEMINIST BASTARD.
EH?!
FEMINIST?
YOU'RE WEAK FOR THEM.
YOU DON'T WANT TO GIVE THEM UP.
WHAT...
YOU'RE OKAY WITH THEM SEEING THIS?
CREASE
SHOCK
BAM
びろーん
YOU JERK OFF TO THIS?
NO, I DO NOT!
LIAR...
THEN WHY DO YOU STILL KEEP STUFF LIKE THIS?

ZOOM.
LIKE THIS.
STUDIO EYE VHS 75min
豐乳さぐ
STUDIO ALFA
渡る世間は乳ばかり
超ハイ
NO...
UM...
I KNOW,
THAT THOSE PORN VIDS HAVE BEEN WITH HIM LONGER THAN I HAVE.
BUT STILL...
MIGHT AS WELL TOSS THEM, IF HE'S GOING TO HIDE THEM LIKE THAT.
THE MAGAZINES, TOO.
OH!
ANIKI!

HEY...
BO ING
...
WHAT?
YOU KNOW, MY FRIENDS CAME OVER.
?
UH-HUH?
WELL ...
MIYUKI'S REALLY INTERESTED IN YOU...
OKAY ...
UH, UM...
THAT MEANS SHE WANTS TO GO OUT WITH YOU.
AH HA HA
WITH ME?
LOTS OF PEOPLE ARE INTER-ESTED IN HER.
TALENT SCOUTS LOOK AT HER, TOO...

DOES SHE HAVE BIG BOOBS?
HUH?!
WELL...
SHE'S MORE ON THE SLENDER SIDE...
SO SHE'S FLAT CHESTED?
EH?
THAT'S NOT TRUE EITHER!!
HUH...
BOOBS...
I'LL THINK ABOUT IT...
SO HE'S INTO THAT...
BOOBS...
FLAT CHESTED...
THAT WAS WEIRD.
I HATE BOOBS.
Sweet
summer

RUMBLE
RUMBLE
STARE
HEY...
MASASHI!
?
WHAT THE HELL ARE YOU DOING?
YOU WERE BOTHERING HER!
HOW?
IT WAS SO OBVIOUS...
I'M EMBARRASSED FOR YOU.
SO?
I WASN'T LEERING OR ANYTHING.
SHE WAS SHOWING THEM OFF ANYWAY.
SHOWING OFF, HUH...

I GUESS SO...
IT WAS HARD TO LOOK ANYWHERE ELSE...
SCRATCH
EXCEPT FOR MY HUGE COCK, RIGHT?
HU...?!
HMPH
AREN'T YOU EMBARRASSED...
GAH...
IT'S HUGE IF IT'S AN INCH BIGGER THAN YOURS.
...
SHRUG
ぶんぶん
ANIKI!
IPPACHI-SAN!
NACCHAN?
ARE YOU TWO HERE FOR THIS MOVIE, TOO?

OH, INTRODUCTIONS.
THIS IS MIYUKI.
NICE TO MEET YOU! ♥
I TOLD YOU ABOUT HER.
YEAH...
...
HEY.
WHY DON'T WE WATCH IT TOGETHER?
!
GREAT IDEA!
...
UM... SHALL WE?
ONII-CHAN ...

MEN'S RESTROOM
男子➡
御手洗し
...
DON' WORR
YOU'RE A GOOD GUY.
BUT YOU'RE TOO NERVOUS ...
NERVOUS?
YOU HAVEN'T SAID A WORD TO HER.
THERE'S NOTHING TO TALK ABOUT.
WHAT'S THERE TO SAY DURING A MOVIE?
OH YOU...
YOU KNOW WHAT I MEAN.

WELL, YOU GO TO AN ALL BOYS' SCHOOL.
BUT YOU'LL GET IT.
SNICKER
SHE WON'T LIKE YOU IF YOU DON'T TAKE ADVANTAGE OF THE MOOD, YOU KNOW.
YOU'RE GIVING *ME* ADVICE?
WHAT ARE YOU THINKING?
SHOCK
WHAT...
I'VE NEVER BEEN WITH A GIRL.
SO WHAT?
WHAT ARE YOU PISSED ABOUT...
I DIDN'T MEAN ANYTHING...
I WAS JUST...
*HOW MANY HAVE YOU BEEN WITH?*

WELL?
HOW MANY HAVE YOU SLEPT WITH?
WHEN WAS YOUR FIRST TIME? WHERE?
WHAT KIND OF WOMAN?
...
WHY ARE YOU ASKING THIS?
ANSWER ME.
A GIRL WITH BIG TITS, RIGHT? HOW MANY DID YOU FUCK?
TWITCH
"FUCK"?

FIVE.
WHAT ABOUT IT?
AND LET ME JUST TELL YOU. I DON'T MESS AROUND WITH THEM.
"FUCK"?
DON'T USE THAT DIRTY WORD FOR THEM.
SO...

WHAT AM I TO YOU?
IF YOU'RE SERIOUS ABOUT US...
WHY DO YOU ACT LIKE YOU DON'T CARE?
!
...
OKAY, I'LL STOP ...
IT'S MY BAD.
SOMETIMES I'M JUST CONFUSED...
ABOUT YOU...
IT'S LIKE YOU'RE A FRIEND, OR A BROTHER...

SINCE WE'RE BOTH GUYS.
YOU COULD BE THE GIRL...
THEN I CAN HAVE YOU.
MASASHI...?!
SLAM
MASA...
LOCK
NN...
BUMP
TCH.
BANG
BANG
御手洗い
MEN'S RESTROOM

CLATTER
?
...!!
RATTLE
RATTLE
SUCK
SUCK
SUCK
LICK
TCH...

-ASTARD...
RATTLE
TCH...
YOU LIKE THAT...?
SUCK
LICK
LICK
SUCK
TWITCH
...CK.
AUGH.
SUCK
LICK
NN...
NGUH...

TRAIL
SLIDE
YOU THINK... I'VE GOTTEN BETTER?
HAA...
AH!
TREMBLE
-SASHI...
WOW.
YOU'RE TWITCHING...
SHAKE
TWITCH
HAA... HA
SLIP
NN...
HA...
STOP...
TELL ME YOU WANT IT...
HA
HA
THE... FUCK...

TELL ME.
RUB
RUB
PUSH
HAA!
AH... AH!
DRIP
HAA...
SMACK
YOU WANT THIS?
TCH...
AH!
IN A PLACE LIKE THIS...
DOING SOME-THING LIKE THIS...
FEEL IT...
JOLT
SHOCK
SHOCK
AHH...!

TWITCH
QUIVER
QUIVER
WHAT IF THE GIRLS SEE YOU LIKE THIS?
AUGH...!
PUSH...
SLIDE
HAA ...!
HA...
KAZUYA...
TCH...
RATTLE
RATTLE
SLAM
SLAM

DON'T YOU FORGET...
I DID A GIRL.
HA
SLIP
HA
YOU THINK...
A GIRL WOULD TAKE YOU LIKE THAT?
TCH...
HA
AHH!
THRUST
THRUST
HAA!
YOU'RE... MINE...
SHOCK
SHIT...
SPURT
SPURT
SPURT
AH...

HAA...
HA ...
I'M NOT...
HAA ...
PANT
PANT
I'M,
NOT A GIRL.
WHY...

HOW COULD YOU SUPPRESS IT?
AH!
WHERE DID YOU GO?! THE MOVIE ENDED...
...?!
WHAT HAPPENED?!
ANOTHER FIGHT?!
SORRY, NACCHAN...
I'M GONNA GO.
EH?
I'LL SEE YOU BACK HOME...!
NO...
HA HA...
IT'S FINE.
BUT...

YOU CAN'T EVEN WALK STRAIGHT.
I'LL GO WITH HER.
AFTER ALL...
OH!
YOU'RE HURT, AREN'T YOU?
...
SINCE WE'RE BOTH GUYS.
UM...
SINCE WE'RE HERE, SHOULD WE FIND SOMETHING ELSE TO DO?
I DON'T MIND...
AH.
YOUR LIPS ARE CUT.
NO...
HERE...
IF YOU'D LIKE...
IT'LL HEAL BY ITSELF...

IPPACHI-SAN?
WAIT ...
IPPACHI-SAN?!
AH...

?!
IPPACHI...
HUH?
HUH?
HEY...
IPPACHI...

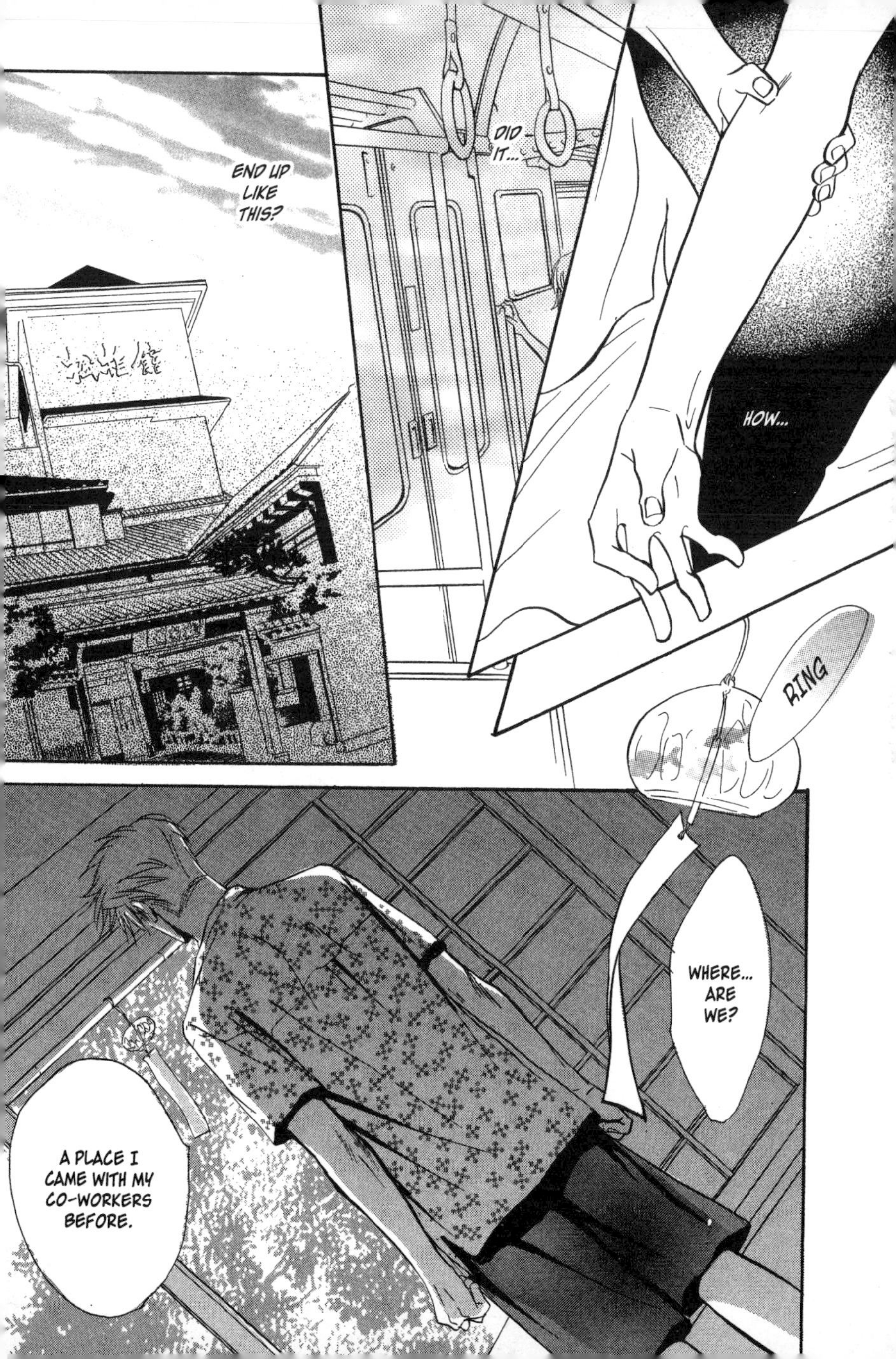
HOW...
DID IT...
END UP LIKE THIS?
RING
WHERE... ARE WE?
A PLACE I CAME WITH MY CO-WORKERS BEFORE.

I DON'T HAVE ANYTHING WITH ME...
HEH...
ME NEITHER.
SO WHAT ARE WE DOING?
YOU DON'T HAVE WORK TOMORROW?
I DO.
AH, I'LL TAKE CARE OF IT.
...
WHY?
SUD-DENLY
ALL THIS...
YOU...

YOU'VE NEVER THOUGHT ABOUT GIRLS BEFORE?
...
NONE, HUH?
NOT ONCE...
NO...
I'VE NEVER THOUGHT ABOUT BEING WITH GUYS EITHER.
UNTIL I MET YOU.
WHY...
IS IT ME?
I WONDER ...

DO YOU WANT A REASON?
RING
I'VE THOUGHT ABOUT IT.
MAYBE IT'S BECAUSE ...
YOU'RE JUST UNCOM-FORTABLE WITH GIRLS.
AND I'M JUST A REPLACEMENT.
IF THAT'S THE CASE,
IT'S NOT FAIR.
FAIR?
I...
DON'T THINK I CAN GO BACK.

I'VE ALREADY PICKED YOU.
I DON'T WANT TO REGRET NOT CHOOSING A GIRL.
KAZUYA...
REGARD-LESS...
WHATEVER YOU WANT IT TO BE, I FIGURED IT WOULD BE YOUR CHOICE.
BUT IN THE END...

WE ENDED UP HERE BEFORE I KNEW IT.
IT'S PROBABLY INSTINCT.

IT CAN'T BE ANYONE ELSE.
MASA... SHI?
GIVE ME A MINUTE ...
NO... BUT TO HAVE MY WILDEST DREAMS COME TRUE LIKE THIS...
WILDEST DREAMS?
I COULD COME JUST BY LOOKING AT YOU.
YOU SERIOUS?
TREMBLE
I WISH I HAD A CAMERA.
SEX IN THESE CLOTHES.
PANT
PANT
THIS GUY...
WHY DID HE PUT HIS GLASSES ON?!

COME ON...
HURRY ...
NUDGE
UGH...
AH...
CREAK
YOU LIKE MY COCK?
UH...?
HA
BETTER THAN BOOBS?
PUSH
THRUST
AH!
NN!
THRUST
AAH!
NN...
WELL?
IDIOT...

IT DOESN'T MATTER ...
AS LONG AS IT'S YOU...
KAZUYA...
THIS IS LIKE...
A SPONTANEOUS HONEYMOON.
ANIKI! IPPACHI-SAN!!

WHERE WERE YOU FOR TWO DAYS?!
IF YOU DIDN'T COME BACK, WE WOULD'VE REPORTED THIS TO THE POLICE!
CRAP... I FORGOT TO CALL.
SKIPPED TWO DAYS.
GEEZ... YOU TWO WERE FIGHTING, THEN YOU GUYS DISAPPEARED...
WHAT IN THE WORLD HAPPENED?
THIS HAPPENED.
OH.
I JUST REMEMBERED.
MAY I BORROW SOME CASH, PLEASE?
HUH?!
WITH THE GIRLS...
THEN HE TOLD ME THEY WENT OFF ON A TRIP!!
CAN YOU BELIEVE THAT?!
HE DIDN'T EVEN CALL!
KNEW IT...
I WAS DUMPED.
SWIVEL
GIVE US ALL THE DIRTY DETAILS!

FREE TALK
WELCOME! ♡ HOW ARE YOU?
CLUB DANDY
HM? YOU DON'T KNOW? PLEASE, FORGIVE ME.

I AM...
YOUR...
SPOTLIGHT
YOUR...
REIJI SAOTOME.
『club DANDY』 HEAD HOST
REIJI SAOTOME (AGE 24)
SAGITTARIUS, BLOOD TYPE AB, LION
(PERSONALITY MATCH)
GABURINCHO!
HUH?! (THOSE WHO GET IT, GET IT.)
"GABURINCHO"
WHAT A NICE LADY.
HA HA HA HA
AKIRA!

SAOTOME WILL SING!
SO CAN I GET A GLASS OF DOM PERIGNON? ♡
UM...
ANYWAY... IT'S NICE TO MEET ALL OF YOU PIERCE READERS!
I REALLY MUST DRAW THIS NEXT TIME... OR SOME-THING...
18+ BOYS LOVE PC GAME
ESCAPE
IS FINALLY ON SALE!
IMPOSSIBLE, TO BE BLINDED BY THIS LOVE... ♫
I FALL FOR IT MYSELF.
OH, EVEN IF THERE'S NOTHING LEFT, THERE WILL BE...
A SAOTOME-LIKE SONG.
VERY SENSUAL VOICE.
BUT CHARACTERS LIKE THEM ONLY BELONG IN GAMES...
ANYHOW, CREATING A BOY'S LOVE GAME WAS A DREAM OF MINE.
SO I'M REALLY HAPPY ABOUT THIS.
SO HE'S A LADY'S MAN?
HE'S SING-ING.
SPACE OUT ...
HE'S REALLY SING-ING...
HA HA
THERE, THERE.
MMHM.
HE'LL SING, TOO.

THERE WILL BE A TOTAL OF TWENTY-ONE OF THEM. (I'M IN CHARGE OF HALF OF THEM)
THE OTHER HALF BELONG TO MY CO-CREATOR!
IT WILL BE FULL OF BOYS!!
NOISE!!
MAKE SOME NOISE!!
AW, FINE... WHOO!
HA HA...
WITHOUT FURTHER ADO, LET'S INTRODUCE THEM!
IT'S COLD SO I'M KEEPING IT ON TODAY. ♪
AQUARIUS, BLOOD TYPE O, CHEETAH (PERSONALITY MATCH)
MOTOKI KAMIJOU, HIGH SCHOOL SENIOR
UPPERCLASSMAN OF THE SWIMMING TEAM
JUN NATSUKAWA
SAME CLASS, IDOL
THE HELL'S WITH THIS SYSTEM?
HISATO YUUKI
LOWER CLASSMAN, FRESHMAN
...
AH... WE'LL HAVE THEM SMILING NEXT TIME...?
IT'S CRAMPED ...
SHIGESHI TOKIWA (AGE 48)
ALGEBRA TEACHER, GENTLEMAN.
TEPPEI FUJISAWA (AGE 28)
MYSTERY MAN, ROUGH.

WANT SOME?

YOSHIHIKO SENA (AGE 23)
PORNO MANGA ARTIST

EHEH

KENSAKU YAMADA (AGE 25)
LEADER, BIOLOGY TEACHER

MAKING EROTIC GAMES IS DEFINITELY THE BEST. I'VE FALLEN IN LOVE WITH THE BOTTOM CHARACTERS.

BUT DRAWING THE TOP CHARACTERS IS EASIER.

PROTAGONIST, YAMATO MAJIMA
HIGH SCHOOL SECOND YEAR,
SAGITTARIUS, BLOOD TYPE AB
JUST EXPERIMENTING, THIS TIME IT'S BLACK HAIR.
HEIGHT IS 5'9"+ (A BIT TALLER THAN SAOTOME (6')?)
HE SEEMS TO HAVE MULTIPLE PERSONALITIES (HAHA) BUT I LIKE IT...
PHEW...
IS EVERYONE HAVING A GOOD TIME?
ESCAPE
FLAP
MERCH! (HAHA)
THERE ARE TEN MORE BESIDES THESE GUYS.
THE BEAUTIFUL SCHOOL COUNCIL PRESIDENT, THE TUTOR'S BROTHER, THE EXCHANGE STUDENT, ETC., ETC....
IS THIS MY HOST CLUB TO ESCAPE REALITY (?).
Yes I Love So!
PROFESSIONAL NAME
AKIRA!
NO... BUT THEN...
THERE'S STILL MORE TO COME...

I DREW A CONSTRUCTION CHARACTER.
AAAAH!
WITHOUT FORGETTING THE SAFETY LINE.
A FOOT ABOVE GROUND.
SCAFFOLDS. OF COURSE HE'S A BOTTOM.
CLICK CLICK
SOUND OF CLICKING
SCAFFOLDS, HUH... I'VE BEEN THERE.
HEH...
IS THIS PART OF SAOTOME'S UNKNOWN PAST?!
THAT WAS A JOKE...
HEH.
I USED TO BE WITH A TALENT AGENCY.
?!
HEH
I'M KIDDING... DON'T LISTEN TO ME.
HEH HEH
GLANCE
!!
WILL THIS BE A BIG SHOW JUST FOR HIM?!

YOU THERE!
ARE YOU INTERESTED IN BEING A HOST?
GRAB
?!
YES...
YOU HAVE THE GOODS.
YOU USE IT MUCH?
GROPE
GROPE
REIJI SAOTOME, SELF-PROCLAIMED AGE OF 24
CRUNCH
GUH...
HE HAS THOSE DAYS, TOO.
DO YOUR BEST, REIJI!

I WILL BE TALKING ABOUT THE GAME HERE. FOR THOSE OF YOU WHO DON'T HAVE A COMPUTER, ARE UNDER 18 YEARS OLD, OR AREN'T INTERESTED, I'M SORRY. WELL, I DID MY BEST WITH THIS OBSESSION OF MINE.

SINCE THIS IS MY FIRST GAME, I BUMPED INTO SOME OBSTACLES, BUT I DID WHAT I COULD WITH THE LIMITED TIME... WITH THAT, I AM SATISFIED. BUT HONESTLY, IT WAS MORE FUN PLAYING IT THAN MAKING IT. THAT'S OBVIOUS (AS WITH MANGA). SO I BECAME A GAMER THIS ONCE AND ENJOYED GAME.

BUT IF YOU HAVEN'T GOTTEN ALL THE CHARACTERS YET... WELL, WHEN YOU DO, YOU GET TO HEAR THE MAIN CHARACTER'S VOICE, SO DO YOUR BEST...

FREE TALK end

KAZUYA SAKAI
LEO, BLOOD TYPE A, TIGER (PERSONALITY MATCH), HEIGHT 5'5"
SHAMELESS - A SCAFFOLD CONSTRUCTOR... I HAD FUN DRAWING HIM AND THE TWO OF THEM TOGETHER. AND MASASHI IS OF COURSE, IS THE MOST PERVERTED CHARACTER I'VE DRAWN THUS FAR.
IT'S BECAUSE HE'S 17? NON! (←THIS IS FROM A MAGAZINE ONE TIME. "BECAUSE THERE'S A HOLE THERE? NON! IT'S BECAUSE YOU WERE THERE!" (HAHA) IT'S GREAT...)
ANYWAY, I WANT THESE CHARACTERS TO STAND OUT EVEN WHEN I'M 60... EVEN I DON'T KNOW IF THESE TWO WILL KEEP GOING OR NOT. BUT RIGHT NOW I SUDDENLY WANT TO DRAW MORE WITH KOUSEI. ONE DAY... (HAHA).
MASASHI EZUMI
CAPRICORN, BLOOD TYPE B, WOLF (PERSONALITY MATCH), HEIGHT 6'1"
FINALLY... FOR THOSE WHO STAYED WITH ME ALL THE WAY HERE,
THANK YOU SO VERY MUCH!
IT MAKES ME SO HAPPY.

Even though Azuma's "spectacle fetish" is infamous, guys are out of the question, and Sorachi is definitely way out of the question - he's too serious for him to even carry on a decent conversation with. Then one day, Azuma finds Sorachi asleep without his glasses, and can't help himself from kissing him!

Tamiya meets Tohdou at Teinou University, a school for kids from well-off families. Tamiya is shocked at the different values that Tohdou and his friends have, but begins a curious friendship with them. As graduation nears, the two friends strike up a fledgling love.

Poor Mizuki is molested on the train on his way to school. But then he finds out the culprit is the student council president?!

Gifted with intelligence and looks, student council president Azuma confessed his love to Mizuki, and with a little push, they "successfully" started dating. The entire school has even officially recognized their relationship. So you would expect things to be progressing smoothly...

# Presents...

Since the student body president's confession of love, Mizuki's been swept up in Azuma's frantic pace. But it seems he's not happy with that?!

Azuma's full-throttle lovey-dovey actions with Mizuki give rise to four stories in the super-popular school love comedy.

Yamaguchi and Takagari have recently gone from close friends to boyfriends. All is well, but Yamaguchi is worried. Takagari seems to love him...too much?! That in itself wouldn't be a bad thing, if it wasn't for the fact that everyone else might find out they're a couple! A striking tale of hidden love!

Yoshinaga's genius and his gift for political maneuvering have helped him ascend to the higher spheres of the Ministry of Foreign Affairs at an early age. As for Shiraishi, his family's prestige, as well as his dedication to his job, has also led him to an early career in diplomacy. When the two meet in Thailand, a stunning tale of love unfolds.

Gentle and delicate convenience store clerk, Kenji, has fallen in love... not with someone who matches his personality, but with a rude construction worker, Kousei, who's in it more for his body than for his feelings.

Love is Like a Hurricane Volume 3

by Tokiya Shimazaki

LOVE CIRCUMSTANCES

by Momoiro Renaijijyo

The Prime Minister's Secret Diplomacy

by Youka Nitta

MAYBE I'M YOUR STEPPIN' STONE

by Shiuko Kano

801 Media Inc.
"THE TRUE GENTLEMEN'S CLUB"
WAHHH! THE END OF THE BOOK ALREADY?
Join our monthly newsletter.
Read 801-chan's insider blog!
Get books directly from us and feel the love!
Discuss the book in our forums.
Don't forget our online store!
Plus we have the cutest packaging imaginable!
801ちゃん
山田ぼたん
801
www.801media.com
© 2006 Yamada Botan

**801-chan Says!**

**"Manga reads from right to left, not the usual left to right you may be familar with.**

**So unless you want to spoil the ending, flip me over and start from the other side!"**

## TRANSLATION AND EDITOR'S NOTES

***PAGE 6***

THE NAME, KAZUYA, CAN ALSO BE READ AS "IPPACHI". MASASHI IS REPLACING IT WITH "IPPATSU" WHICH MEANS "ONE KISS/ONE TIME" AS A PUN.

***PAGE 10***

*NAME A KIND OF CELL. A JAIL CELL.*

THE REAL JOKE (IN JAPANESE) IS A PUN INVOLVING A JAPANESE PERSON'S NAME.

***INSIDE DUST JACKET FLAP***

ABE NO SEIMEI IS A HISTORICAL AND LEGENDARY FIGURE IN JAPANESE FOLKLORE. HE WAS THOUGHT TO HAVE MYSTICAL POWERS AND NOW THERE IS A SHRINE FOR HIM IN KYOTO.

**Thanks for reading with us!**

**• 801-chan**